INSURANCE LEARNERS

PROPERTY AND PECUNIARY INSURANCE

by

MARK DACEY

GW00702290

LONDON
WITHERBY & CO. LTD.
32-36 Aylesbury Street,
London EC1R OET
Tel No. 01-251 5341
Fax No. 01-251 1296

1st Edition 1985

Reprinted 1987

2nd Edition 1989

MONUMENT
SERIES

©

WITHERBY & CO. LTD.

1989

ISBN 0 948691 85 9

CONTENTS

INTRODUCTION

"Insurance Learners" are a valuable aid to the study of the Qualifying Examinations of the Chartered Insurance Institute.

Students in other fields of professional study (banking, accountancy, etc) have at their disposal, in addition to main texts, "slim volumes" which, ideally, serve both as preliminary **reading** and **revision** texts. Insurance Learners aim to fulfil a similar function for CII students. **The Learner will help the student to organise his thoughts and gain insight into the study material before moving on to the main text** which should be studied more effectively as a result. Once the study of the main text has been completed it is suggested that frequent revision should be undertaken with the aid of the Learner, the presentation of which is designed to facilitate such an approach. The publishers recommend that Learners are most effectively used when the main text is that which has been published by the CII Tuition Service to fulfil the requirements of the same syllabus.

In this Learner questions from previous examination papers are set out, by kind permission of the Chartered Insurance Institute, in Appendix 1. Questions are grouped according to topic areas but some questions, of course, ask the student to bring in aspects of a number of topics. The student is advised to draw up framework answers to ALL questions and convert as many as possible to fully written solutions. It is above all the desire of INSURANCE LEARNING SYSTEMS to encourage a systematic approach to study along with the development of sound examination technique.

How the "Learner" should be used

The "Learner" is more than just a crammer — rather it is a succinct complement to a planned programme of study and a valuable revision aid. You should:

1) Locate the topic to be studied in the "Learner" and read it.

2) Read the topic as covered by the main CII textbook and as directed by the lecturer if attending a class.
   Note taking from the main text, and during oral tuition should be easier and more effective now that the "Learner" has opened up the topic area.

3) Re-read the topic in the "Learner", revising frequently from your notes and the Learner.

4) Attempt "framework" answers to ALL questions in Appendix 1 converting as many as possible into full solutions. Discuss your work with others.

THE GROUNDWORK

The CII identifies three levels of knowledge:

1) 'BE AWARE OF'

2) 'UNDERSTAND'

3) 'THOROUGHLY UNDERSTAND'

At Associateship level we are concerned with levels 1 and 2.

'BE AWARE OF' implies a general knowledge of facts which should be treated in a descriptive manner.

'UNDERSTAND' implies a particular knowledge of facts and an ability to present reasoned arguments involving their application in given circumstances.

Clearly this is an important distinction for students of Property and Pecuniary Insurance. We do not have to demonstrate the same degree of knowledge of all the different aspects of this course, rather we can focus attention initially on the 'UNDERSTAND' topics and consider those 'BE AWARE OF' features as a secondary function.

THE SYLLABUS

Property and Pecuniary Insurances

AIM: To build upon and extend the student's knowledge and understanding of the general theory and practice of insurance as applied to property and pecuniary insurances.

We need to 'UNDERSTAND':

1) The demand for property and pecuniary insurances.

2) How the principles of insurance apply to property and pecuniary insurances.

3) The scope of the following classes of insurance:

Fire	"All Risks"
Additional Perils	Theft
Household	

4) The bases for fixing sums insured and how these are related to methods of calculating premiums and settling claims; the problem of value; full insurance and first-loss insurance; average conditions.

5) The methods and applications of reinsurance in relation to property and pecuniary insurances.

We need to 'BE AWARE OF':

1) The scope of the following classes of insurance:

Credit	Contingency
Interruption	Engineering
Fidelity Guarantee	Livestock
Legal Expenses	

2) The role of the insurance market in the provision of bonds and other forms of financial guarantee.

3) What property and what pecuniary risks may be insured, who may insure them and against what perils, and what perils are uninsurable.

4) The role of the insurance market in risk improvement and loss prevention.

3.10 **The two conditions of average**
This is concerned with a situation where property may be insured under more than one policy. It sometimes happens that there is a **specific** policy covering goods which might also be insured under a **general** policy. The first of the two conditions is the straight-forward pro rata condition. The second condition allows that a more specific policy pays first in the event of a loss. Any uninsured portion of the specific policy will fall to the general policy which effectively pays second. The amount falling to the more general policy is itself subject to the pro rata condition of average.

REINSTATEMENT

3.11 Insurance policies are designed to pay money to compensate for loss but there are three circumstances under which reinstatement — payment of money to achieve the physical restoration of the property — may take place:

(i)   by insurers under the terms of the policy

(ii)   by insurers under statute

(iii)   by the insured under statute or perhaps by contract.

3.12 **Reinstatement under the terms of the policy**
The operative clause of e.g. a fire policy gives insurers the **option** to reinstate rather than pay money in the event of a loss. The option must be exercised within a reasonable time and once it has been taken cannot be revoked. If an insurer fails to reinstate adequately then he is liable for damages for breach of contract. Despite these difficulties an insurer may decide to reinstate if he suspects a fraud to gain policy monies. Another reason for reinstatement is claims cost saving. Some property has a large retail 'mark-up' e.g. jewellery. By purchasing at wholesale price and providing reinstatement insurers can settle a claim cheaper than by providing the retail price.

3.13 **Reinstatement by insurers under statute**
Insurers can become bound to ensure that insurance monies are expended upon reinstatement (of buildings only) under the terms of the Fires Prevention (Metropolis) Act 1774. This can arise in two ways:

(i)   when there is reason to believe fraudulent intention, insurers are obliged to ensure that insurance monies are spent on reinstatement.

(ii)   when insurers are requested to reinstate by any person with a qualifying interest in a property e.g. lessees, mortgagees, tenants, then the Act says insurers are required "to cause the insurance money to be laid out and expended (on reinstatement)".

In the eighteenth century fire was a dreadful thing in towns and cities and could easily spread from house to house. The only effective way to prevent its spread was the blowing-up of properties in its path. Just as arson is a serious cause of fires in industrial properties today, so was it a much more serious cause of spreading fires in private houses in 1774. Owner-occupation was unkown in those times except in the case of some mansions owned by the wealthy. The intention of the Act therefore was to protect the occupier and others against fires by arson.

3.14   Reinstatement by the insured

An insured client may be forced to reinstate under statute or perhaps by contract. The provisions of the Trustee Act 1925 and the Law of Property Act 1925 both allow that the insured must use insurance monies on reinstatement. In contract law an insured may be a tenant with a provision in his lease obliging him to insure the property and to use policy monies on reinstatement.

3.15   The reinstatement memorandum

This is the clause that allows 'new for old' cover rather than settlement on an indemnity basis where deduction is made for wear and tear. The clause is seen on policies covering buildings, contents and machinery but not stock. Points arising are:

(i)   The clause only applies if the property is actually reinstated.

(ii)   Reinstatement work must be started and completed reasonably quickly.

(iii)   The sum insured must be adequate with a special proviso relating to average. If the sum insured is 85% or greater of the value at risk at the time of reinstatement then no average applies.

3.16   The impact of inflation

Inflation caused grave problems for the insurance industry and particularly for policies written on a reinstatement basis. The physical process of reinstatement could take months or even years from a loss that happened during the last few days of a policy period. By the time reinstatment was under way, inflation could have rendered the sum insured quite inadequate, hence the relaxation of average on these policies to the 85% rule mentioned above. Other mechanisms were developed to address this problem as follows:

3.17   The Escalator Clause

The insured chooses a rate of inflation expressed as an annual percentage rate e.g. 12%. The clause allows that the sum insured is increased over the policy period by that percentage and an additional premium is chargeable on 50% of the consequent increase in sum insured. This system is used in insurances on buildings and contents but not stock (which is covered under a declaration policy).

3.18   The Valuation Linked Scheme

This system allows for inflationary increases affecting buildings or machinery during the period of reinstatement as well as during the policy period. The insured chooses an inflation rate for the policy year and for each of the years during which reinstatement work will be carried out. These rates are applied on a compound basis to the original sum insured or base value, e.g.

Base Value	£1,000,000
Selected inflationary rate for policy year (15%)	150,000
	1,150,000
Selected inflationary rate for reinstatement year one (12%)	138,000
	1,288,000
Selected inflationary rate for reinstatement year two (10%)	128,800
Sum Insured	1,416,800

The difference between the Base Value and the Sum Insured of £416,800 is the inflation provision. This is charged at 70% of the full premium rate. It is essential that the Base Value is accurate and therefore it must be certified by a qualified, professional valuer as adequate. Full average applies at the time of reinstatement.

3.19 **Adjustable Premium Policy Scheme**
This sytem embraces buildings worth over £1 million insured on a reinstatement basis. Again the sum insured is a base value and an inflation provision but the premium is restrospectively adjusted at each renewal to reflect actual inflation rates. The maximum return premium is 50% and again base values must be certified by qualified, professional valuers. Full average applies at the date of loss.

3.20 **Notional Reinstatement Value Scheme**
Again the sum insured is in two parts, the declared value and the inflation amount which is to allow for increase during both the policy and reinstatement periods. The declared value is the figure the insured calculates as adequate for reinstatement at inception of the policy — the notional reinstatement value. The policy is prepared showing three figures: the sum insured, the declared value and a percentage figure for inflationary increase. A professional valuation is not required as such but makes good, commercial sense.

3.21 **Day one basis of reinstatement cover**
Again the system allows for a two-part sum insured; the declared value and the added provision for inflation. The declared value is updated at each renewal of the policy. Here the insured does not have to select an actual inflation rate. It is essential that the sum insured at inception is adequate (average applies on this figure). The insured can then pay a flat rate of 15% above normal terms for the cover or a rate of 7.5% above normal adjustable at the end of the policy period on the increased declared value.

3.22   **Valued Policies**

Some categories of property provide particular difficulties of accurate valuation. Such property includes antiques, works of art and veteran or vintage cars. For this property a valued policy may be issued with an agreed amount as the sum insured which is payable in the event of a total loss. The agreeed amount is normally certified by a qualified valuer at the inception of the policy. The principle of indemnity is not violated by these policies as long as a bona fide valuation is used. The policy is made void by significant over-valuation. In the event of a partial loss, the policy reverts to an indemnity basis.

3.23   **First Loss Policies**

An insured may have property of such a nature that it could virtually never all be lost in one claim. An example might be a theft risk where the stock is a large amount of metal which it would be physically impossible for thieves to remove at one time. The sum insured under a first loss policy represents less than the amount at risk but a figure considered adequate to cover any likely loss.

First loss policies are cheaper than those on full value, hence the attraction to the insured client. The insured must declare what is the full value at risk however, as this is a rating consideration. A form of average applies to ensure that full value is declared:

$$\frac{\text{Declared Value}}{\text{Actual Amount at Risk}} \quad \text{x} \quad \text{First Loss}$$

CHAPTER 4

RISK REDUCTION AND LOSS PREVENTION

4.01   Risk improvement is concerned with two main concepts:

(i)   The likelihood of a loss occurring in the first instance (the inception hazard).

(ii)   The extent of the loss development possibility following an occurrence (the development hazard).

Accordingly risk assessors or surveyors who have specific expertise in their fields (fire, theft, engineering, etc) attempt to identify hazards in these two areas. Similarly insurers become involved in research and prevention organisations bearing upon both the incidence and extent of losses.

4.02   Hazard can be categorised into physical and moral. **Physical hazard** concerns the inherent features of a risk: the construction of a building in a fire insurance or the nature of the stock in theft insurance. Has the building got a thatched roof? Is the stock particularly attractive to thieves e.g. cigarettes? **Moral hazard** describes those features of a risk arising from the involvement of people in that risk: the trade might be dubious e.g. amusement arcade or the workforce of an organisation might be employed on a casual basis.

4.03   Hazard can also be considered in terms of general features and specific features. General hazards for example in fire insurance will concern the construction and location of the premises, the system of heating and the standard of the electrical system in operation. Specific hazards will cover the nature of the operations within the premises. Is the trade-process dangerous in that it involves the application of heat? Are flammable/combustible materials used or stored? Does the process produce dangerous by-products?

4.04   In addressing an examination question on this topic, it is essential to produce an **organised** answer in order that the candidate may be successful in covering all the points. We can go on to consider risk reduction and loss prevention in the main categories of property and pecuniary insurance.

FIRE INSURANCE

4.05   **General Physical Hazards** These will concern:

Construction	—	are there any undesirable features such as large amounts of wood? Is the building compartmentalised to provide fire breaks?
Location	—	is the building in a remote place many miles from the nearest fire-brigade? Is it in a run-down district of a town or city? Is it adjacent to buildings where particularly hazardous processes are conducted or goods are stored?

Heating — is the system safe? Are there any portable heaters such as paraffin stoves?

Electrical — is the system appropriate for the risk? Is it in a modern, safe condition?

Tidiness — untidy premises offer both inception and development hazards. Waste material or packing material lying around provides a place both for fires to start and a means of spreading.

4.06 **Specific Physical Hazards** These will concern:

Trade — is the trade hazardous? Does it involve the application of heat? Are all the processes stable and capable of being controlled?

Raw materials — are they flammable or combustible e.g. cellulose paints and thinners, plastics etc?

By-products — does the trade process generate dangerous by-products such as vapours, unstable materials and the like?

4.07 **Moral hazard.** This will concern:

Housekeeping — are the premises maintained in good order, well-lit and reasonably clean and tidy? Is the machinery properly maintained and used according to specification?

Management — is there evidence of poor management e.g. bad employee relations, slap-dash methods of operation, inadequate supervision of workers and the like.

Employees — is the workforce stable and reasonably happy or is there evidence of unrest e.g. vandalism.

4.08 **Protections** These include:

— fire alarms and smoke detectors
— fire extinguishing appliances
— bans on smoking
— fireproof doors and compartments
— automatic sprinkler installations.

4.09 **Bodies connected with research include:**
The Fire Protection Association (F.P.A). This body is supported by insurers and provides technical advice, publicity material and education about fire protection. Research covers building materials, industrial processes, fire prevention and fire containment. A large number of publications are produced providing both general and specific guidance in the fire prevention field.

4.10   Fire Insurers' Research and Testing Organisation (F.I.R.T.O.). This body is financed by insurers and is concerned with testing construction of buildings and building material. It also tests extinguishing appliances. It reports upon the results of its tests and therefore provides information about the suitability of construction materials and effectiveness of fire fighting equipment.

4.11   Central Fire Liaison Panel (C.F.L.P.). This body was set up in 1967 to co-ordinate on a national basis the efforts of regional fire panels. Again the idea is involvement and discussion on fire prevention matters with the promotion of fire prevention ideas and general education of fire-awareness amongst appropriate organisations.

4.12   The Fire Research Station is part of the Building Research Establishment of the Department of the Environment. Investigative work is conducted upon buildings and building materials, fire protection devices and extinguishment systems. Further, statistics are gathered and maintained on all fires attended by fire brigades.

4.13   When the A.B.I. was reformed another change was the creation of the Loss Prevention Council or L.P.C. This is an independent body using the resources of four of the pre-existing insurance funded organisations i.e. F.P.A., F.I.R.T.O., the Insurance Technical Bureau and part of the Fire Offices' Committee (F.O.C.).

THEFT INSURANCE

4.14   **General Physical Hazards** These will concern:

Construction   —   is the building stout enough to be reasonably thief-resistant or is it of dangerously light construction e.g. a sports pavilion? Are the doors and windows of a reasonably strong nature or perhaps rather flimsy?

Location   —   is the building in a remote place which would allow thieves unobserved access? Is it in a run-down part of town?

Communication   —   is the building self-contained or is the risk part of multi-occupied premises? Self-contained theft risks are generally a much better proposition.

4.15   **Specific Physical Hazards.** These will concern:

Goods   —   is the property to be insured attractive to thieves e.g. jewellery, furs, cigarettes, wines or spirits?

Portability   —   can the goods be fairly easily removed e.g. cigarettes (which are also of course easily disposable)

Ease of entry   —   are there many points of access — doors, windows and skylights? Are these means of access protected by locks, bolts, bars and grilles?

| Previous loss record | — | an underwriter will always want to know what has happened in the past. In theft insurance this is a question of obviously crucial importance. |

4.16 **Moral hazard.** This will concern:

Trade	—	some trades can give rise to difficulties e.g. fancy goods dealers, scrap-metal merchants and the like. An underwriter will always be particularly anxious about involvement in a theft risk of this nature.
Housekeeping	—	Similar points arise to those mentioned in connection with fire insurance. Are the premises maintained in good order, well lit and reasonably clean and tidy? Are locks maintained in good condition.
Management	—	here a surveyor would look for evidence of responsible attitude. Is the management security conscious? Again are employee relations good and supervision adequate?
Employees	—	similarly to Fire Insurance, is the workforce stable and reasonably content or are there indications of unrest?

4.17 **Protections** These include:
— locks, bolts, bar grilles
— burglar alarms
— safes, strongrooms, secure areas
— night watchmen, security patrols
— floodlighting of premises at night

4.18 **Bodies connected with research include:**
The Association of Burglary Insurance Surveyors (A.B.I.S.). As the name implies this is a collection of persons with a specific interest in theft insurance. Work embraces research into theft protection and promotion of anti-theft ideas in general.

4.19 The National Supervisory Council for Intruder Alarms (N.S.C.I.A.). This organisation has as its objective the creation and maintenance of a high standard of alarm systems and membership is open to those alarm installers who meet specific standards of operation.

4.20 The Police Force also contributes in this sector by the provision of Crime Prevention Officers who offer specific advice on combating theft and attempt to educate the public on theft matters in general.

ENGINEERING INSURANCE

4.21   Again the position here is different because an Engineering Surveyor is concerned with both an ordinary assessment of risk from an insurance standpoint and with the extra dimension of compulsory inspection of certain categories of plant. Essentially the survey is concerned with the age and state of the machinery or equipment and the likelihood of its failure.

4.22   'Protections' are concerned with good engineering practice and therefore policy conditions exclude testing of machines, the application of abnormal loads upon machines or their use outside the scope of their specification. These factors together with identification of any developing faults as a result of survey work are the main techniques for risk reduction and loss prevention.

4.23   There are no specific central research bodies as such, but large insurers have their own research stations and maintain close liaison with manufacturers and universities.

CONSEQUENTIAL LOSS INSURANCE

4.24   Here insurers need to be aware of both inception and development hazard in the first instance but are then concerned with the **interruption risk.** These policies pay for the consequence of an interruption to a business and so the objective is to ensure, if at all possible, that the insured does not have 'all his eggs in one basket'.

4.25   Is it possible to split the means of production into two separate centres so that if one is inoperative after a loss, the other can, by shift-working or overtime, make up some of the shortfall in production? Are reciprocal arrangements possible with other organisations whereby, for example, computer-time sharing is available in an emergency? Is the insured dependent upon a single machine — if so are there any ways in which a replacement machine could be acquired quickly or should the machine be specially protected against loss?

4.26   In consequential loss insurance the surveyor must identify the interruption features — those aspects of a risk which in the event of a loss are going to cause difficulties in resuming production. Interruption features vary according to the trade under consideration.

FIDELITY GUARANTEE INSURANCE

4.27   Here insurers compensate an employer for losses as a result of dishonesty of his employees. As part of the underwriting process the insurer will investigate the employee and the system of operation in force. Both these techniques contribute towards loss avoidance. Checking upon the employee ensures no undue exposure to a loss arising from a moral hazard. Checking the insured's system of operation ensures that no weaknesses exist which could be dishonestly exploited. Fidelity Guarantee insurers have many years of experience and will readily identify weaknesses in any system of operation.

EXAMINATION CONSIDERATIONS

This element of the course concerns an essentially practical subject and has produced a number of examination questions over the years. It is important to construct a methodical framework to address such questions. This framework, as we have seen, embraces the following features:

General Physical Hazards
Specific Physical Hazards
Moral Hazard
Protections
Research Organisations.

In some instances, the examiner will actually provide a description of a risk in the question. Read and consider such questions carefully because all the details will be relevant. Then go on to apply a **methodical** approach in your answer.

Past questions on this subject are reproduced in the Appendix at the back of the book.

CHAPTER 5

THEFT INSURANCES

5.01   In this section we will consider:

Theft insurance
'All Risks' insurance
Money insurance
Goods in Transit insurance

N.B. Theft and 'All Risks' are topics which we need to 'UNDERSTAND'.

5.02   **Theft Insurance**

Business premises theft policies cover theft **involving entry to or exit from the premises by forcible and violent means.** The intention is to provide cover only against 'break-in' types of loss. Wider cover would provide problems of the enormous extent of losses and proof of loss in such a situation, for example as sneak-theft or pilfering.

This is a most difficult class of business for insurers. Briefly the underwriting considerations are:

(i)   degree of attraction of the goods

(ii)   portability of the goods

(iii)   protections on the premises

(iv)   nature and location of the premises

(v)   previous loss experience.

Underwriters will usually require the completion of a proposal form and a survey of the premises. Very often cover will only be granted subject to improvements in security.

In addition to theft losses, these policies cover damage to the building and contents consequent upon theft or attempted theft. The **exceptions** are:

(i)   loss or damage by fire

(ii)   damage to stained plate or decorated glass

(iii)   loss by any person lawfully on the premises or brought about with the connivance of an employee or family member.

(iv)   loss of or damage to money, securities, coins, medals, stamps, precious stones, documents, business books, manuscripts, computer systems records, curios, sculptures, rare books, patterns, models, moulds, designs, tobacco, cigars or cigarettes unless specially mentioned as being insured. (This is a similar exclusion to that found in a fire policy and is there for the same reason. The problems are proof of value, proof of loss and degree of hazard).

5.03   **Policy conditions**

Points to note in particular are:

Exclusions
Claims condition
Cancellation condition

Exclusions — Radioactive risks
War risks

No claim is recoverable if there is any change made in the premises or condition of the risk (This allows for either increased hazard or reduced security).

Claims condition — identifies what steps the insured must take in the event of a loss, including advising the police.

Cancellation condition — allows insurers to cancel the policy by giving seven days notice by registered letter to the insured. (This is an extreme measure but insurers reserve this right on all particularly hazardous forms of business).

5.04   **'All Risks' Insurance**

This is the widest form of cover and the easiest way to remember what is the cover is to identify the **exclusions:**

(i)   Radioactive risks

(ii)   War risks

(iii)   Riot, civil commotion, earthquake or volcanic eruption **outside the U.K.**

(iv)   Delay, confiscation or detention by Custom House or other officials or authorities

(v)   Wear and tear, depreciation, gradual deterioration, moth, vermin or any process of cleaning, dyeing or restoring

(vi)   Damage or breakage of brittle articles **unless** caused by fire, theft or attempted theft

(vii)   Electrical or mechanical derangement.

Provided a loss does not arise from any of these seven points, then it is covered under an 'all risks' policy. The rate of premium is high as it reflects the wide range of cover. A valuation would be required for particularly expensive items.

5.05   **Geographical limits are:**

Great Britain
Ireland
Northern Ireland
Channel Islands
Isle of Man.

5.06   **Pairs or sets clause**

This used to be included on 'All Risks' policies and it limited a loss of part of a pair, or set, to its pro rata value of that set. A pair of vases might be worth £1000 together but one vase on its on might only fetch £350. In the event of a loss the pairs or sets clause determined that only £500 would be payable for the loss of one vase **not** the extra £150 loss as a result of the end of the set.

5.07 In the past 'All Risks' cover has embraced valuable items such as jewellery, furs, photographic equipment and the like. Nowadays there is an industrial form of 'All Risks' cover issued by fire insurers. This, despite its name, does not provide nearly so much cover as that outlined above.

5.08 **Money insurance**

'Money' includes: cash, bank and currency notes, cheques, postal orders, national savings and holiday with pay stamps and luncheon vouchers.

Cover is provided on an 'all risks' basis in seven categories:

(i) In actual transit (carried by the insured, his representative or sent by post).

(ii) In a bank night-safe.

(iii) On the insured's premises during business hours.

(iv) In a locked safe or a strongroom outside business hours.

(v) On the insured's premises outside business hours but **not** in a safe or strongroom (this cover is normally limited e.g. £250).

(vi) In the private residence of the insured or any of his employees (again cover limited to e.g. £250).

(vii) In the custody of collectors or travellers (normally a twenty-four limit applies here).

5.09 **Points to note**

(i) Safes and strongrooms normally have a limit imposed upon them as to the maximum insured amount they may contain.

(ii) The policy covers damage to safes and strongrooms caused by theft or attempted theft.

(iii) Personal accident benefits can be added for carriers of money who may be attacked.

(iv) There is usually a **key-clause** requiring that all keys to safes and strongrooms be removed from the business premises outside business hours.

(v) Premium is calculated on the amount of money carried during the year with an adjustable, deposit premium charged.

5.10 **Geographical limits are:**

Great Britain
Ireland
Northern Ireland
Channel Islands
Isle of Man.

5.11   **Exclusions are:**

Radioactive risks
War risks
Dishonesy of an employee not discovered within seven days
Confiscation, nationalisation, requisition or wilful destruction by the authorities
Shortages due to error or omission
Losses recoverable under a fidelity guarantee policy
Losses due to depreciation (e.g. currency fluctuation)
Losses from unattended vehicles
Contents of coin-operated machines.

5.12   **Goods in transit insurance**
This cover is on an 'All Risks' basis and covers goods whilst in transit anywhere in Great Britain. Like most other aspects of theft cover, it is a difficult account to underwrite. Cover includes goods during loading, carriage, unloading or temporary garaging of all vehicles and trailers. Two main types of policy are issued:

(i)   covering an insured's own vehicles with a sum insured per vehicle

(ii)   covering all goods dispatched by the insured on his own or road hauliers' vehicles, goods carried by rail or goods sent through the post. Here there is a sum insured per consignment.

5.13   **Excluded property is similar to that on other policies:**

explosives, acids and goods of a dangerous nature
bullion, cash, bank and currency notes
deeds, bonds and securities
jewellery and precious stones
clocks, watches and antiques
business books, moulds, patterns and designs
livestock.

(Again the reasons for exclusion are hazardous nature, proof of loss, particularly attractive goods and brittle articles).

5.14   **Exclusions are:**

Radioactive risks
War risks
Theft or pilferage by the insured's employees
Samples accompanying commercial travellers
Moth, vermin, insects, damp, mildew or rust
Delay, deterioration and changes by natural cause.

EXAMINATION CONSIDERATIONS
This is another important section of the course. Learn the basic structures of these policies and see the Appendix for the type of questions which can arise in this sector.

CHAPTER 6

ENGINEERING INSURANCE

6.01   There are four principal headings under which plant may be grouped:

(i)   Boilers and pressure plant

(ii)   Engine plant

(iii)   Electrical plant

(iv)   Lifting machinery.

6.02   **Boilers and pressure plant**
This category includes superheaters, economisers steam baking ovens and any other pressure vessels. Indemnity is provided against damage to the boiler **and surrounding property** consequent upon explosion or collapse.

Explosion   —   is the suddent and violent **rending** of the plant by force of internal steam or other fluid pressure causing bodily displacement of any part of the plant, together with forcible ejection of the contents.

Collapse   —   is the sudden and dangerous **distortion** of any part of the plant caused by crushing stress by force of steam or other fluid pressure.

The intention is to provide cover against a specific incident rather than any gradually operating cause such as cracks, fractures, blisters, corrosion and the like.

6.03   **Engine plant**
This category includes steam-engines, gas and oil engines, diesel engines, air compressors and refrigeration equipment. Indemnity is provided against mechanical breakdown **and damage to surrounding property** caused by flying fragments.

In both categories above an unusual feature arises in that in addition to indemnity for the item of plant that is insured, cover is also provided for damage to surrounding property. This gives rise to a problem in that the insured must select an adequate sum insured to pay for such damage. Calculation of an adequate sum insured is a difficult process.

6.04   **Electrical plant**
This category includes electrical motors, generators, transformers, turbines and the like. Indemnity is provided against mechanical or electrical breakdown.

6.05   **Lifting machinery**
This category includes cranes, hoists, passenger or goods lifts and all lifting gear **irrespective** of motive power. Indemnity is provided against breakdown.

INSPECTION SERVICE

6.06   The position with regard to the surveying of engineering plant is unusual. In addition to inspection for normal insurance purposes of risk assessment and loss avoidance, the inspection service satisfies statutory requirements. Various Factories Acts, and more recently the Health and Safety at Work Act 1974, have laid down requirements for the inspection 'by a competent person' of some plant. Cranes must be inspected at least every 14 months. All other lifting appliances must be inspected at least every 6 months. Boilers and pressure vessels must be examined at least every 14 months. Inspection services are also available for both engine and electrical plant. There is no **legal** compulsion for this, but from an operator's point of view it makes good commercial sense to have such plant regularly checked. From an insurers's point of view, inspection of such plant may be a prerequisite to granting cover.

If the inspection service is provided by an independent contract then the fees chargeable would attract V.A.T. In practice many engineering policies provide both insurance cover and the inspection service for a single premium. In these cases the Customs and Excise authorities have agreed that such premiums would be exempt in full. It therefore makes good sense for the client to have a single contract for both insurance and inspection services.

EXAMINATION CONSIDERATIONS

Cover under engineering insurance policies is a subject that we must 'be aware of'. Full questions are rare but a number of part questions have been asked as can be seen in the Appendix. The candidate needs to have an outline knowledge of this subject for examination purposes.

CHAPTER 7

FIRE INSURANCE AND ADDITIONAL PERILS INSURANCE

7.01   Remember these are two topics we must 'UNDERSTAND'. They make regular appearances in the examination.

7.02   Cover is provided under a standard fire policy in respect of three perils:

> fire
> lightning
> explosion.

These perils are covered as follows:

7.03   **Fire** is actual burning damage following ignition. Most proximately caused damage is also covered such as loss as a result of water used in fire fighting, damage done by the fire brigade, property destroyed to prevent fire spread and the like.

7.04   **Exceptions**

(i)   **Its own** spontaneous fermentation.

(ii)   **Its** undergoing any process involving the application of heat.

(iii)   Earthquake.

(iv)   Subterranean fire.

(v)   Riot or civil commotion.

(vi)   War, invasion, act of foreign enemies, hostilities (whether war be declared or not) civil war, rebellion, revolution, insurrection or military or usurped power.

7.05   Note in exceptions (i) and (ii) the emphasis on 'its own' and 'its'. It is only the **individual item** that spontaneously ferments or undergoes the application of heat which is excluded from the cover. Fire damage spreading from that incident is covered.

7.06   The Public Order Act 1986 redefined riot and created a new crime of violent disorder. The requirements for riot are now:

(i)   The number of people must not be less than twelve.

(ii)   They must use or threaten unlawful violence for a common purpose.

(iii)   The conduct is such as would cause a person of reasonable firmness present at the scene to fear for his own personal safety.

7.07   **Lightning**
All lightning damage is covered whether there is a fire or not.

7.08   **Explosion**
There is a limited amount of cover only provided by a standard fire policy. Concussion damage is covered:

(a)   of boilers used for domestic purposes only

(b)   in a building (not being part of any Gas Works) of gas used for domestic purposes or used for lighting or heating the building.

With the exception of (a) and (b) above, there is no concussion damage cover provided under a fire policy but the rules of proximate cause with regard to fire damage are amended. There are three possible combinations of fire and explosion:

(i)   Explosion followed by fire. No concussion damage (unless it is (a) or (b) above) but fire following explosion is specifically **included** in the cover.

(ii)   Fire followed by explosion. Fire damage is covered but again concussion damage even though proximately caused by fire is specifically **excluded.**

(iii)   Explosion damage without fire. Again unless it is (a) or (b) above it is specifically **excluded.**

7.09   **Policy Conditions**
Points to note in particular are:

Exclusions
Claims condition
Insurer's rights after a fire
Arbitration

7.10   **Exclusions:**

(i)   Radioactive risks.

(ii)   Goods held in trust or on commission, money, securities, stamps, documents, manuscripts, business books, computer systems records, patterns, models, moulds, plans, designs or explosives.

(iii)   Property insured under a Marine policy.

7.11   **Claims condition:**
This lays out the detail of what the client must do in the event of a claim. It is a condition precedent to liability under a policy.

7.12   **Insurers rights after a fire**
This condition specifies that insurers are allowed to enter or take possession of the damaged building and may deal with goods and property in any reasonable manner.

7.13 **Arbitration**

This condition allows that in the event of a dispute about the amount to be paid under a policy (not about liability under the policy) then arbitration proceedings must precede an action in court.

There are of course other policy conditions but generally these are concerned with amendment of common law conditions and restatement of implied conditions.

7.14 **Additional Perils Insurance**

These perils can be added to the cover of a standard fire policy and they include:

    Aircraft
    Explosion
    Riot or Civil commotion
    Malicious damage
    Storm or tempest
    Flood
    Burst or overflowing of water tanks, apparatus or pipes
    Impact.

7.15 Aircraft perils are planes or other aerial devices, or articles dropped therefrom, excluding pressure waves caused by devices travelling at sonic or supersonic speed.

7.16 Explosion perils are exclusive of boilers and pressure vessels (which are insurable under an engineering policy) and are over and above the limited amount of cover provided by a standard fire policy. This cover is needed where there is the possibility of dust explosions such as in corn mills or explosion of flammable vapours such as in paint factories. The rate for the risk will depend upon the degree of exposure.

7.17 Riot and civil commotion perils are fairly standard but some premises will be more exposed to hazard than others e.g. property adjoining a football ground.

7.18 Malicious damage cover has similar considerations to those mentioned above in connection with riot and civil commotion. This peril is covered in addition to riot and civil commotion and excluded are loss by theft, loss through confiscation, destruction or requisition by order of the Government, loss or damage resulting from cessation of work and destruction or damage whilst the premises are untenanted or vacant.

7.19 Storm or tempest risks vary enormously and need individual underwriting consideration. This primarily concerns the age and state of the buildings and their exposure to storm damage as a result of their location.

7.20 Flood risks again need individual underwriting consideration which hinges upon the location of the buildings and the previous loss record.

7.21   Bursting or overflowing of water tanks, apparatus or pipes cover is granted provided the buildings are in a reasonable condition. Another underwriting consideration is whether the contents of the building are particularly susceptible to water damage e.g. cigarettes.

7.22   Impact damage by any motorised vehicle, horses or cattle is another peril, and it can include damage arising from the insured's own vehicles, for the payment of an extra premium.

7.23   **Special conditions**

Riot damage claims can be made against the police force responsible for the area in which the damage occurs. A claim must be made within fourteen days, and so insurers always require notification from their client within seven days so that they can instigate a subrogation recovery from the police.

Malicious damage claims must be immediately reported to the Police Authority as well as to insurers.

The water perils (storm, tempest, flood and burst pipes) all have a (say) £100 excess for each and every loss. It is also a condition for these covers that the premises, water tanks, apparatus and pipes be maintained in a good and substantial state of repair.

Storm and tempest perils do not include flood, inundation from the sea, frost, subsidence, heave or landslip. Destruction or damage to fences, gates or property in the open is also excluded.

Flood does not include damage to fences, gates or property in the open nor damage by frost, subsidence, heave or landslip.

Bursting or overflowing of water tanks, apparatus or pipes does not embrace leakage from an automatic sprinkler installation. Damage whilst the premises are unoccupied is also excluded.

There is usually a £100 excess on impact damage from the insured's own vehicles.

EXAMINATION CONSIDERATIONS

This is an extremely important part of the course which regularly produces examination questions. It is essential that the candidate knows the cover under a standard fire policy and what the special or additional perils are. For examples of questions that have arisen, see the Appendix at the back of the book.

CHAPTER 8

FURTHER FEATURES OF FIRE INSURANCE

8.01 The previous chapter concentrated upon the cover under fire insurance. There are a number of other features to consider and in this chapter we will consider:

Declaration Policies
Sprinkler Leakage Insurance
Collective Policies
Long Term Agreements
Architects' and Surveyors Fees
Public Authorities Clause
Removal of Debris.

8.02 **Declaration Policies**

These policies cover stock and are designed to allow an insured to maintain full insurance on fluctuating stock values, without over-insuring and therefore paying too much premium. The insured selects the maximum amount at risk and pays a deposit premium of 75% based on this value. He then declares the actual amounts at risk monthly, or quarterly, (depending on policy conditions) throughout the period of insurance. At the end of the period the average declaration is calculated, as is the appropriate premium. This premium is compared with the deposit charged at the beginning of the period and an adjusting additional or return premium is calculated. The maximum additional or return premium allowable is 33.333% of the deposit charged. Declarations must be made within 30 days of the specified date, and late or no declarations are deemed to be declared as the maximum sum insured, as are over-declarations.

Declaration policy questions are very straight-forward if the candidate adopts a methodical approach:

(i)   Take the sum insured, apply the rate of premium to get a figure.

(ii)   Take 75% of that sum which is the deposit premium chargeable.

(iii)   Add the declarations together.

N.B.   Over declarations) Are deemed to be the
       No declarations   ) maximum sum insured.

(iv)   Divide the total of declarations as appropriate (by twelve for monthly declarations or by four for quarterly).

(v)   Apply the rate of premium to the average declaration figure produced in (iv) above.

(vi)   Compare the premium in (v) with that in (ii). Calculate the difference, which is either an additional premium or a return premium. (Remember the additional or return premium cannot be greater than 33.333% of the deposit charged).

8.03   This question appeared in 1977:

'The following figures were submitted under a fire policy for stock insured on a declaration basis with a sum insured of £150,000. The policy provides for declarations to be made monthly and it is subject to the normal declaration conditions:

1.1.76	£125,000	1.7.76	£145,500
1.2.76	£120,800	1.8.76	£130,600
1.3.76	No declaration	1.9.76	£145,900
1.4.76	£ £85,500	1.10.76	£139,500
1.5.76	£ 84,325	1.11.76	No declaration
1.6.76	£140,000	1.12.76	£133,275

The policy is renewable at Christmas and the gross rate is 0.20%. Calculate the premium adjustment which would have been made at Christmas 1976.'

Step 1   £150,000 @ 0.2% = £300.00

Step 2   75% of £300.00   = £225.00
                          Deposit chargeable

Step 3   £125,000
         £120,800
         £150,000   (maximum deemed declared)
         £ 85,500
         £ 84,325
         £140,000
         £145,500
         £130,600
         £145,900
         £139,500
         £150,000   (maximum deemed declared)
         £133,275
         ‾‾‾‾‾‾‾‾‾
         £1,550,400
         ‾‾‾‾‾‾‾‾‾

N.B.   There were no-over declarations in this question. If there had been, these would have been reduced to £150,000.

Step 4 £1,550,400 divided by 12	=	£129,200
Step 5 £129,200 @ 0.2%	=	£258.40
Step 6 Premium earned	=	£258.40
Deposit premium paid	=	£225.00
Additional premium payable		£ 33.40

8.04   **Sprinkler Leakage Insurance**

This risk may be covered by a separate policy or sometimes by an extension to the Special Perils cover. An automatic sprinkler system is a good form of protection against fire damage providing, as it does, water under pressure very quickly in response to the start of a fire. A problem arises however in that having a building covered by a series of pipes and sprinkler heads means that there is a risk of water damage if the installation is accidentally damaged by, for example, a fork-lift truck. Another danger is water freezing in the pipes. A sprinkler leakage policy pays for damage from the accidental discharge of water from the system. Exclusions are:

(i)   Heat caused by fire.

(ii)   Repairs or alterations to the buildings or premises.

(iii)   The sprinkler installation being either repaired, removed or extended.

(iv)   Freezing whilst the premises are empty or disused.

(v)   The order of the Government or of any municipal, local or other competent authority.

(vi)   Earthquake, subterranean fire riot, civil commotion and war risks.

(vii)   Explosion, the blowing-up of buildings or blasting.

(viii) Pressure waves caused by aircraft or other aerial devices travelling at sonic or supersonic speeds.

8.05   **Collective Policies**

These are encountered regularly in fire insurance and constitute an effective way of dealing with risks too large for any one insurer. Normally the company with the largest percentage of the risk will be the **Leading Office** and it will prepare copy documentation for the insurers with smaller percentages: the **co-insurers.** Co-insurers signify their acceptance of the documentation and authorise the Leading Office to sign a collective policy on their behalf by the issue of a **signing slip** to the Leading Office.

This system has administrative advantages of uniformity of wording for a risk and cost-saving, in that one collective document is cheaper to produce than a series of individual documents.

8.06   **Long-Term Agreements**

Once a policy has been issued it is to the Insurer's advantage to maintain renewal of that policy, as renewal is cheaper administratively than issuing new policies. Long term agreements are separate contracts where in return for a discount off premium, the insured agrees to renew the policy with the insurers for a specific number of years. Examples of Long Term Agreements are:

5% discount for 3 years

7.5% discount for 5 years

As long as the insurer maintains the same terms and conditions of cover at renewal then the insured has contracted to renew the policy. The insurer is not bound to offer renewal terms and if he offers amended terms then the insured may avoid renewal. If however the insurer does offer renewal at unaltered terms and the insured does not renew, then in theory the insurer could sue the insured for breach of contract.

8.07   Architects' and Surveyors' Fees
In the event of a loss there will be fees incurred in repairing the damaged building. Such fees are not automatically covered under a fire policy unless there is a clause specifically including them. Fees can be insured under a separate item on the policy or included in the sum insured on buildings. If the latter, then the sum insured must be adequate to cover both the buildings and the fees.

8.08   Public Authorities Clause
In the event of a loss and the need to repair or reinstate a building, a local authority may take the opportunity to insist upon certain alterations or improvements being incorporated in the reinstatement. This clause allows for the costs of such requirements to be met by the fire policy provided the sum insured is adequate. Remember that the clause only operates if there has been a loss under the policy.

8.09   Removal of Debris
Normally the cost of debris removal is met by a fire policy but in certain circumstances there may be extra debris removal charges arising from the nature of the risk. A damaged building may block a road or waterway for example. The debris removal clause allows for the payment of such extra cost. Again there can be a separate item added to a policy or the costs can be included in sums insured on other items. Either way the sum insured must be adequate to meet the costs.

EXAMINATION CONSIDERATIONS
It is important to know the contents of this section. Part questions have arisen on these topics in the past, as can be seen in the Appendix.

CHAPTER 9

HOUSEHOLD INSURANCE

9.01 It is difficult to talk in general terms about household policies nowadays because there is not really any such thing as a 'standard' policy. The household tariff was dissolved in the late 1960's and before that time one could talk about a standard wording. Since then however, insurers have significantly increased the cover that they offer under these policies as part of their marketing effort. Different companies have emphasised different aspects of cover and so policies have evolved differently.

A big problem in the household market has been widespread under-insurance particularly as a result of inflationary price rises. Most insurers now insist upon 'index-linked' policies where the sum insured is automatically increased in line with the Index of Retail Prices. This is not a complete answer to the problem of under-insurance but it has alleviated some of the worse effects.

9.02 Policies are available separately for buildings and contents or on a combined basis. Cover is very wide indeed:

Buildings embraces all of the property including outbuildings, walls, fences and gates. The perils are:

> Fire, lightning and explosion
> Riot, civil commotion and malicious damage
> Aircraft
> Storm, tempest and flood
> Subsidence and landslip
> Theft or any attempt thereat
> Bursting or overflowing of water tanks, apparatus or pipes
> Impact with the buildings by any road vehicles, horses or cattle
> Breakage or collapse of television or radio aerials
> Leakage of oil from any fixed oil-fired heating installations
> Loss of rent
> Accidental damage to service pipes and cables
> Breakage of fixed glass and sanitary fixtures
> Property owner's liability.

9.03 **Points to note**

(i) Some perils are not operative if the house is left unfurnished:

> Theft or any attempt thereat
> Burst pipes
> Malicious damage
> Breakage of glass and sanitary fixtures.

37

(ii)   The water perils (storm, tempest, flood and burst pipes) and malicious damage peril have a compulsory excess e.g. £15.

(iii)   The subsidence and landslip peril has an excess normally of £250 or 3% of the sum insured, whichever is the greater.

(iv)   Loss of rent includes ground rent and is insured normally for a maximum of 10% of the sum insured.

9.04   **Contents** embraces household goods and personal effects of every description belonging to the insured or to members of his family permanently residing with him. The perils are:

> Fire, lightning and explosion
> Riot, civil commotion & malicious damage
> Aircraft
> Storm, tempest and flood
> Theft or any attempt thereat
> Bursting or overflowing of water tanks, apparatus or pipes
> Impact by any road vehicle, horses or cattle
> Leaking of oil from any fixed oil-fired heating installations
> Breakage of mirrors & glass in furniture
> Loss of rent
> Occupier's liability
> Escape of water from heating installations or washing machines
> Accidental damage to television sets
> Deep-freeze contents loss through accidental failure of
> the electricity supply or contamination by refrigerants
> Accidental damage to drain inspection covers, drain
> and sewer pipes.

9.05   **Points to note**

(i)   There is no excess in respect of the water perils but there is an excess e.g. £15 in respect of Malicious Damage and Accidental Damage to drain inspection covers, etc.

(ii)   Property **temporarily** removed (other than for sale or in furniture depositories) is covered subject to the following limitations:

There is no cover in respect of Storm, Tempest and Flood for property in transit.

Theft is only covered:

In transit to a bank or safe deposit
In a bank or safe deposit
At a private dwelling
At the insured's place of work or where he is resident.

(iii)   Cash, currency or bank notes and stamps are insured for a maximum of £50.

(iv) Excluded property is deeds, bonds, bills of exchange, promissory notes, cheques, securities for money, documents of any kind, manuscripts, medals, coins, motor vehicles and livestock.

(v) There is a single article limit of 5% of the total sum insured on contents.

(vi) The total value of precious articles is considered not to be greater than 33% of the sum insured on contents.

(vii) Theft is part qualified by the 'forcible and violent entry' proviso. Theft is only covered if accompanied by forcible and violent entry:

Of cash, currency notes, bank notes and stamps.

In a building not solely occupied by the insured.

All other theft losses are covered **without** the forcible and violent entry proviso.

(viii) Loss of rent is again limited to 10% of the sum insured (on contents).

EXAMINATION CONSIDERATIONS

The range of cover under household policies is very wide indeed and it does vary from insurer to insurer. Accordingly we might expect examination questions on the main sections of the cover e.g. theft of contents. Study the past questions indicated in the Appendix to get an idea of the sort of question that has arisen in the past.

CHAPTER 10

REINSURANCE

10.01　This is a topic which we need to 'UNDERSTAND'.

Reinsurance is a risk-spreading technique that supports the essential nature of insurance — the widespread sharing of risks. Clearly it is in an insurer's interest to be involved in a small extent in a large number of risks than to be exposed to large losses in a small number of risks.

Once they have accepted a risk, insurers themselves have an insurable interest in that risk and therefore can reinsure. It is important to remember that reinsurance is an entirely separate contractual arrangement from the original insurance policy, and therefore in English and Scottish law there can be no legal relationship between the original insured and the reinsurer. Each has an independent contract with the insurer.

10.02　Reinsurance can be considered as proportional and non-proportional. In proportional the reinsurer(s) have, as the name implies, a specific fixed interest in a risk. Non-proportional cover embraces an aspect of the original insurer's business, possibly just one case, but more likely a whole account.

Proportional cover can be facultative or Treaty. Treaty can be further subdivided into Quota Share, Surplus and Facultative Obligatory. **Non-proportional** cover embraces Catastrophe Excess of Loss, Working Excess of Loss and Stop Loss or Excess of Loss Ratio reinsurance.

10.03　**Facultative**

This is the oldest form of reinsurance. Having acquired a risk direct, an underwriter would attempt to hive-off a proportion of that risk to a facultative underwriter. If he succeeded in placing say 35% of the risk on a facultative basis then he would pass over or **cede** 35% of the premium on that risk and cover 35% of any claim.

Facultative reinsurance worked well but had administrative problems. Dealing with reinsurers on a one-for-one basis for every risk became an expensive process because there was the need for telephone calls and forms for every transaction. Accordingly **Treaty** arrangements were set up to counter this difficulty.

10.04　A reinsurance treaty is an arrangement whereby a reinsurer agrees for a period of time (usually one year) to accept a portion of all risks within a certain category of business and subject to various conditions. This has the advantage that once agreement has been reached, an insurer can automatically cede business to the treaty without reference to reinsurers. The problem from a reinsurer's point of view is obvious. He is dependent upon the insurer for the results of the treaty and for the quality of business ceded thereto.

10.05   **Quota Share**

Under this arrangement an insurer is bound to cede a fixed proportion of all risks within the agreed category to reinsurers. Quota share arrangements are therefore expressed as percentages, e.g. 50% quota share, 35% quota share and so on. The insurer passes the appropriate percentage of all premiums to reinsurers and recovers that percentage of all claims.

The advantages of a quota share treaty are that they are cheap and easy to operate and there is a common interest between the insurer and the reinsurer in the operation of the account. Because he is bound to cede a fixed percentage, the insurer cannot select which risks he will or will not pass over to the reinsurers.

10.06   **Surplus Treaty**

This arrangement does allow an insurer a degree of selection in placing reinsurance to the treaty. A surplus treaty works on the basis of **lines.** A line is the amount that an insurer retains for its net account which will vary from risk to risk according to quality e.g. a Fire account might have a minimum line of £12,000 and a maximum of £120,000. The minimum risk might be a plastics factory and the maximum an office block. A surplus treaty is expressed in multiples of lines e.g. a ten-line treaty or a twelve-line treaty and so on. The capacity of the treaty therefore has a direct relationship to the retention of the ceding office, which can pass the surplus of a risk in excess of its own retention to the surplus treaty, subject to the capacity of the surplus treaty.

Example: An office has a twelve-line treaty and a retention of £15,000. The maximum risk it can accept therefore is:

Retention	£ 15,000
Treaty (12 x retention)	£180,000
Maximum gross acceptance	£195,000

Again premiums are passed to reinsurers in proportion to the amount of risk they have accepted and claims are paid by reinsurers in the same way.

10.07   The sort of arrangement described above would constitute a **first surplus treaty.** It is quite possible to have second or third surplus treaties in addition. If these arrangements are in force, then they pick up proportions of a risk after earlier surplus treaties have been filled.

10.08   The reinsurances described above have all been proportional arrangements. In addition to these it is possible to arrange cover on a non-proportional basis. These reinsurances protect against individual large losses on a whole account rather than a fixed percentage of all claims.

10.09   **Catastrophe Excess of Loss**

Insurers might be exposed on many individual risks to loss as a result of a single event, e.g. major storms or flooding. By paying a percentage of the premium income of the underwriting account which they wish to protect, they can purchase reinsurance which will pay up to an amount of money **in excess** of a figure chosen by the ceding office. An insurer may decide that the maximum loss it wants to pay from one event might be £100,000. It may have some idea of what its exposure to loss from one event might be, but will not usually have detailed knowledge. Accordingly it will purchase catastrophe excess of loss protection over £100,000 up to the figure it considers represents its exposure e.g. £400,000 excess of £100,000 which presumes a maximum catastrophe loss of £500,000. It may purchase layers of protection e.g.:

Layer 1   £400,000 excess of   £100,000

Layer 2   £500,000 excess of   £500,000

Layer 3   £1,000,000 excess of £1,000,000

The further away from the bottom, the lower the percentage of premium income payable for the cover.

10.10 Working (or Underwriting) Excess of Loss

This provides an alternative to proportional reinsurance. It operates on the same basis as catastrophe excess of loss but with much lower excess points. This means that the reinsurance is called upon to pay individual losses, hence the name 'working' excess of loss. The problem for reinsurers in this form of cover is the possibility of selection against them. Accordingly levels of cover and rates of reinsurance premium have to be very closely monitored.

10.11 Stop Loss or Excess of Loss Ratio

This form of reinsurance is designed to protect against wild fluctuations in an insurer's loss ratio in any one year. A reinsurer, in return for a proportion of the premium income of an underwriting account, will pay a proportion of a loss ratio in excess of a figure chosen by the insurer. An insurer may select a 90% loss ratio and purchase stop loss protection which will pay 75% of any loss ratio on the account between 90% and, say, 150%.

Cover would never be granted for 100% of the excess loss ratio and there are always upper limits beyond which reinsurers will not pay (in our example 150%). An insurer could however purchase further layers over and above 150%). Again the rate of premium charged depends upon the percentage figures selected and the loss record of the insurers.

EXAMINATION CONSIDERATIONS

It is important to know not only about the methods of reinsurance, but how they actually work. Past questions have involved calculations which really are quite straightforward, provided the basic details are understood. See the Appendix for examples of past questions.

CHAPTER 11

CREDIT AND LEGAL EXPENSES INSURANCE

11.01 **Credit Insurance** aims to indemnify against loss arising as a consequence of a buyer's inability to pay for goods sold to him on credit. However, it does not indemnify against loss of profit. For this reason, and to ensure that the insured is careful about whom he allows credit, the policy never covers 100% of the amount at risk. There is always **co-insurance** between the insurer and the insured on credit policies.

Underwriting consideration embraces the following factors:

The type of trade or business
The length of credit allowed
The spread of the credit risk
The previous loss record of the insured
A general view of the quality of the insured's accounts and system of credit control.

Premium is charged as a rate % on turnover. Policies are available in two main forms:

Specific amount policies, as the name implies, cover known danger spots. These covers are tantamount to selection against the insurer and therefore are rated very highly.

Whole turnover policies, again as the name implies, cover the whole credit risk of an organisation (subject to the co-insurance factor mentioned above) at an average rate of premium.

11.02 **The Export Credit Gaurantee Department** (ECGD) is a Government Department which also provides credit insurance. In addition to commercial failure, cover is also provided against loss due to economic or political frustration of payment. Further, cover is available against expropriation of overseas assets.

The benefits of credit insurance are significant. ECGD covers encourage the export of goods and overseas investment by removing the consequences of a major possibility of loss. Commercial credit insurance protects the one major asset which is regularly uninsured: trade debtors. In doing this it can restore working capital lost through bad debts and provides an effective alternative for the maintenance of bad debt reserves.

11.03 **Legal Expenses insurance** is a relatively new form of cover which has seen significant growth in recent times. It is available on a personal or corporate basis and aims to indemnify the insured against the cost of fighting or defending legal actions. In addition, a corporate policy protects against damages awarded for unfair dismissal. Because the cover is relatively new, it varies from insurer to insurer, but typically, it would embrace:

(i)   Costs of defending an action under the Health and Safety at Work Act 1974.

(ii)   Costs of defending an action under Income Tax or Revenue Laws.

(iii)   Costs of defending a contract of employment dispute.

(iv)   Costs of defending an action arising out of the purchase or supply of goods or services.

(v)   Costs of pursuing third parties for damage to the insured's goods, property, premises or business.

(vi)   Costs of defending criminal prosecutions.

(vii)   Compensation for loss of wages/salary if any member of the workforce has to attend a court, tribunal or arbitration hearing.

(viii)   Compensation for awards of damages to an ex-employee for unfair dismissal.

11.04   Exclusions are:

(i)   Losses incurred prior to written acceptance of a claim by the insurer.

(ii)   Losses where the case is defended without the insurer's approval or other than as recommended by the appointed solicitor.

(iii)   Losses where the insured has failed to give instructions in a timely manner to the appointed solicitor.

(iv)   Losses where the insured causes a delay prejudicial to the defence.

(v)   Fines.

11.05   Book Debts Insurance

The loss of accounting records (by fire or other perils) can create a significant financial loss. This is because the insured will be unable to identify his debtors and there will be a consequent non-payment of outstanding debit balances. These policies cover the shortfall in debt payment following the destruction of records. They do **not** however cover bad debts (that is the province of credit insurance).

Every month (within 30 days) the insured declares what is the total of outstanding debit balances. The premium is charged at a rate per cent per annum on the average amount declared. Book debts are not covered by a standard consequential loss policy because they were incurred **before** the date of the damage.

EXAMINATION CONSIDERATIONS

We need to 'BE AWARE OF' the scope of Credit, Legal Expenses and Book Debts insurances. A question was asked on Credit and Legal Expenses in 1984 and it seems unlikely that this area will see a question every year.

CHAPTER 12

FIDELITY GUARANTEE AND CONTINGENCY INSURANCES

12.01   **Fidelity Guarantee** insurance is issued to commercial organisations to indemnify an employer against direct pecuniary losses and losses of stock through acts of dishonesty by employees.

12.02   **Types of policy are:**
>Individual
>Collective (Named)
>Collective (Un-named)
>Blanket
>Positions

12.03   In an individual policy one named employee is covered for a specific amount. Collective policies cover a number of employees, either on an individual amount per person or category, or for an overall amount for all insured personnel. Blanket policies cover all personnel and a Positions policy covers office rather than a named individual. Four forms are used in arranging cover:

12.04   **Applicant's form:**
asks about the name, address, age, salary and financial status of the employee. Details are required of any past guarantee and previous employment.

12.05   **Employer's form:**
this is virtually the proposal form and asks about the systems in force, details of checking and internal audit, the manner in which cash is handled and details of any previous losses.

12.06   **Private reference form:**
is a standard document whereby the applicant gets two or more friends or acquaintances to vouch for him. It is not much use in practice.

12.07   **Previous employer's form:**
is sent to all employers for the previous five years and asks about the applicant's history with those employers. It provides useful information.

12.08   Underwriting considerations include a system of working, the system of checking, the nature of supervision and the previous loss record of the insured. Fidelity Guarantee insurers are vastly experienced and may make suggestions for improvement as a prerequisite to the granting of cover.

12.09   **Discovery period**
It may be that a loss could be discovered long after it was perpetrated by the employee. Accordingly, there is always a 'discovery period clause' in fidelity insurances which limits claims payable to those discovered within certain time parameters. Examples would be claims not payable:

(i)   Discovered later than twelve months after the resignation, dismissal or death of the employee responsible.

(ii)   Discovered later than six months after the termination of the policy.

12.10   **Court bonds** are needed to ensure that no possibility of loss can arise when the courts appoint people responsible for the safe-keeping of other individual's property. **The Court of Protection** may appoint a receiver to manage the estate of someone who is insane, or senile and not capable of managing their own affairs. To protect against possible loss, the receiver must take out a **Court of Protection Bond.** This would protect the estate against any loss arising through the receiver's maladministration.

A judge may appoint a receiver for a minor or property subject to litigation. Again the receiver will administer the estate and must take out a bond to guarantee the security of the estate. Such arrangements are **Chancery Guarantees.**

The Administration of Estates Act 1971 identified circumstances in the administration of estates where a guarantee was required. Broadly, these are where administration is granted to an individual with some sort of interest in the estate.

12.11   **Government bonds** fulfil a similar function to court bonds: the guarantee of payment (in the event of some happening to frustrate payment) of revenue due to H.M. Customs and Excise. The best example is the removal of goods from a bonded warehouse without the payment of excise duties. In this eventuality, a **General Warehouse Bond** or a **Removal Bond** would ensure that excise duties were paid.

12.12   **Bankruptcy and liquidation bonds** are needed to guarantee a trustee in bankruptcy appointed by the creditors. The trustee has control of the bankrupt person's assets and in the event that the trustee fails to carry out his duties correctly, the bond will make good any loss suffered by the estate.

12.13   **Local Government bonds** are needed in respect of all accounting and clerical staff employed by local authorities. These covers parallel commercial fidelity guarantees taken out by private sector organisations.

EXAMINATION CONSIDERATIONS
We need to 'BE AWARE OF' the scope of Fidelity Guarantee and Contingency Insurance and the role of the insurance market in the provision of bonds and other forms of financial guarantee. Questions do arise in this sector e.g. Question 6 in 1983 as indicated in the Appendix. It does seem unlikely that this area will see a question every year however.

CHAPTER 13

BUSINESS INTERRUPTION INSURANCE

13.01 This form of cover is also known as Loss of Profits or Consequential Loss insurance. It is concerned with paying for the **consequence** of a material damage loss. Accordingly, indemnity is provided against loss of net profit and standing charges (those which still have to be paid even if a company is not earning) as a result of an interruption to the business following a loss.

13.02 **Underwriting considerations**

The underwriter is concerned here with factors which will contribute towards increasing the length of time between a loss and a resumption of work: the **interruption features.** He is after all paying the client for the interruption period and therefore wants it to be as short as possible. Main factors in risk assessment:

(i) The type of risk. Some enterprises will be capable of being restored quickly, e.g. a small shop or service business. Others by their very nature are large, complicated risks which in the event of a loss will generally take a long time to re-establish e.g. a motor car manufacturer.

(ii) The spread of risk. If a manufacturer has just one point of production then that is a bad interruption feature. If manufacture takes place over two or more premises then a loss at one may be offset to some degree by increased production at another. Very simply, we want to avoid 'all the eggs in one basket'.

(iii) Dependency. If an organisation is totally dependent upon one feature e.g. the computer or a central warehouse then that constitutes a poor interruption feature.

(iv) If a business is seasonal then a loss just before the best period of trading may result in a disproportionately large claim compared with a non-seasonal trade.

(v) Speciality. The business may require a special building and/or unique machinery for production. In the event of a loss, it would take longer to replace them then 'standard' buildings or machinery, therefore the interruption would be longer.

(vi) Competition may be fierce. In the event of an interruption, an organisation might lose trade to a competitor and not recover it when it restarts production. It follows that the consequences of interruption would last longer in these circumstances.

Definitions

13.03 **Gross profit** is the main item insured under an interruption policy. It represents the net profit and expenses which still have to be paid even if the concern is not trading (the standing charges).

13.04   **Turnover** is the income of the business which may arise from sales of goods or services, fees or rent.

13.05   **Indemnity period** is the time selected by the client, which is considered to be the maximum period it would take following a loss to get back into full production. This will vary from 3 or 6 months for a small simple business, to 3 or 4 years for a complex manufacturing concern.

The formal definition of Indemnity Period is:

'the period beginning with the occurrence of the damage and ending not later than — months thereafter during which the results of the business shall be affected in consequence of the damage.'

13.06   **The Business** is defined as described by the insured and it is important that it embraces all sources of revenue-earning if the policy is to provide full cover. If, for example, an organisation let off part of its premises and earned rent, then it should include in 'the business' the activity of landlords in addition to its main pursuit. In this way the rental income would be covered by the policy.

13.07   **The premises** are also described by the client and similar considerations apply. The definition must include all sources of revenue if they are to be covered under the policy.

13.08   **Rate of Gross Profit** needs to be calculated in the event of a loss. Quite simply, this is the amount of net profit and standing charges added together compared to the turnover. In the event of an interruption, turnover reduces and the policy pays an amount produced by applying the rate of gross profit to the reduction in turnover.

13.09   **Increase in Cost of Working** is something else that is payable by a consequential loss policy. Very often, by paying extra costs, a shortfall in production can be reduced. If an organisation manufacturers at two premises and one is lost, then by paying overtime rates and bonuses it may be possible to increase production at the other. Such costs are payable under a consequential loss policy **provided** they are cost-effective. The amount paid for increased cost of working must be equal to or less than the loss of gross profit thereby avoided.

13.10   **Auditors' charges** constitute another item that can be covered under a business interruption policy. In the event of a claim the cost of calculating and submitting details of the loss fall on the insured. These costs can be insured under the auditors' charges item.

13.11 **Calculating the Sum Insured**

This is achieved by the 'difference' basis, taking figures from the insured's profit and loss account.

13.12 **Gross Profit** is the amount by which:

Turnover + Closing Stock + Work in Progress

exceeds

Opening stock + Purchases + Specified
(uninsured) Working Expenses

Five out of six figures are lifted straight from the profit and loss account although the descriptions of the items may vary slightly e.g. Turnover may be referred to as 'Sales'. The main interpretive process at this stage is identifying the Specified (uninsured) Working Expenses. These are items which vary according to production and therefore are not payable (and do not need to be insured) in the event of an interruption. They may be described in the profit and loss account as 'Variable Charges' which makes identification very easy. In a more detailed account the most likely examples of specified working expenses are Carriage, Packing and Freight, Discounts Allowed and Bad Debts. As a general rule, if you are in doubt as to whether an item is a specified working expense or not, leave it out of the calculation. Items entered in this category are on the bottom-half of the calculation and thereby **reduce** the sum insured. It is safer to ignore dubious items and over, rather than under-insure.

The actual figure calculated may need further amendment. The profit and loss account is for a past period of trading but the sum insured is to cover the future. You may be told of an expected increase in trading or a percentage inflation rate. Such figures are applied to the Gross Profit sum to increase it accordingly.

The other reason for increasing the sum insured arises from the indemnity period. The figures will be taken from an annual profit and loss account and therefore represent a twelve month period. If the indemnity period is twelve months or less — no adjustment is made. If the indemnity period is greater than twelve months the sum insured must be increased accordingly e.g. x 1.5 for 18 months indemnity period, x 3 for a 3 year indemnity period and so on.

For an example of how this applies in practice we will consider a question from the 1978 examination paper (reproduced with the kind permission of the C.I.I.);

'From the following figures calculate the Gross Profit achieved by the business for the purposes of the normal consequential loss specification wording.

Using the same figures as a guide, and taking into account current business and economic conditions, state what figure you would consider appropriate for a Gross Profit sum insured for a standard policy having a thirty-month indemnity period, explaining the assumptions made in arriving at the figure selected.

Extracted from the 1977 accounts of Cicero & Co Ltd.:

Sales	£250,000
Purchases	£100,000
Fixed charges	£ 70,000
Variable charges	£ 30,000
Stock at 1.1.77	£ 25,000
Stock at 31.12.77	£ 20,000

Gross Profit = the amount by which

Turnover + Closing Stock + Work in Progress

exceeds

Opening Stock + Purchases + Specified Working Expenses.

£250,000 + £ 20,000 + Nil   =   £270,000

£ 25,000 + £100,000 + £30,000   =   £155,000

                                    £115,000

Gross Profit	£115,000
Inflation during policy year (10%)	£ 11,500
	£126,500
Inflation during ind. period year 1 (10%)	£ 12,650
	£139,150 (a)
Inflation during ind. period 2 (10%)	£ 13,915
	£153,065 (b)
Inflation during last 6 months of ind. period (10%) (on half of previous year's figure)	£ ·7,653
Half of previous year's figure	£ 76,532
	£ 84,185 (c)

So we add (a) + (b) + (c) £139,150

                              £154,065

                              £ 84,185

                              £377,400

This approach allows for the fact that any increase factor must be calculated on a **compound** basis''.

Largely because of this problem of having to allow compound elements rather than risk being underinsured, a new mechanism has been introduced. This is the **Declaration Linked** basis of cover. Here the insured establishes a figure which is adequate for the policy year **without** projections for the future. This figure is shown in the policy as **Estimated Gross Profit.** This policy then allows for the sum insured to **increase** by 33.3% of the Estimated Gross Profit figure. The insured has to declare the actual Gross Profit figure at the end of each period of insurance and the premium is adjusted either upwards or downwards. This mechanism is the Business Interruption equivalent of the Day one basis in property insurance. It is anticipated that a 33.3% margin will be adequate for the expansion factor for the vast majority of risks. There is no Average condition on these policies.

13.13 **Wages**

There used to be a distinction between wages and salaries. In the event of an interruption salaried staff would probably be kept in employment with weekly paid staff being laid off. Accordingly, salaries would have been included in the Gross Profit figure as a standing charge and wages would have been excluded as a variable charge or specified working expense.

13.14 In modern times, an employer would hopefully not lay off either category of worker and would therefore insure all remuneration within the Gross Profit item. This is known as **Payroll Cover.** An employer will have union agreements with regard to minimal periods of notice and would anyway not want to lose his skilled workforce in the event of an interruption. For these reasons it seems commercially sensible, as well as socially responsible, to maintain Payroll Cover.

13.15 In between the two extremes outlined above is a form of partial wages cover whereby wages are insured as a separate item on the **Dual Basis.** This allows 100% wages cover for a selected number of weeks and then a selected percentage of the wage roll for the balance of the indemnity period e.g. 100% for the first 10 weeks and 50% thereafter. The system allows an **option to consolidate** which means that the number of weeks of 100% cover can be increased at the cost of abandoning the partial cover. In this example by dropping the 50% cover for the balance of the indemnity period, the 100% period of cover would be increased to 30 weeks. This mechanism is used for partial losses where the interruption lasts longer than the period of initial 100% cover but less than the full indemnity period. It follows that by exercising the option to consolidate, the employer may be able to keep all his workforce employed.

Extensions

13.16 An insured client may be exposed to loss as a result of events other than on his own premises. A component manufacturer may suffer if his major customer has a loss and an interruption meaning that no components are purchased. This eventuality may be insured by a **Customer's Extension.**

13.17 The reverse of this situation will be that the user of the components could experience loss if his supplier had an interruption and was not able to produce. This would be covered under a **Suppliers Extension.**

13.18   A retailer may experience a reduction in turnover if customers are physically barred from entering his premises, for example as a result of emergency repair work to neighbouring buildings. This would be covered under a **Denial of Access Extension.**

13.19   Hoteliers may experience losses arising as a result of murder, suicide, food or drink poisoning at the premises or pollution of the nearby coastline. All these eventualities could lead to cancellations and reduce bookings and can therefore be added to the scope of their consequential loss policies.

13.20   **Points to remember**

(i)   Never reduce the sum insured if the indemnity period is less than twelve months. It is only **increased** for indemnity periods longer than twelve months but is never reduced.

(ii)   All the figures used are taken from previous trading records and the policy insures future trading expectation. This is possible because of the **Special Circumstances Clause** which allows for adjustments to be made for any factors that may have arisen which will have a bearing upon results.

(iii)   Increase in Cost of Working cover under a standard policy must be cost effective before it can be spent. It is possible, however, to have a separate item or policy in respect of Increase in Cost of Working. There are no qualifications in respect of such cover.

(iv)   The sum insured is an estimate of future trading figures so the insured is encouraged to maintain a full sum insured by the Declaration system. This allows up to a 50% return of premium in the event that at the end of the period of insurance the actual Gross Profit is less than the sum insured.

(v)   There is no excuse for under-insurance on a business interruption policy because of the declaration system. Accordingly pro-rata average applies in the event of under-insurance.

13.21   **Advance Profits**
A major development such as the construction of a new brewery (a happy thought) might well take three years to complete. An interruption during construction would mean a delay in the plant coming on stream and therefore a financial loss in the future. Advance profits policies pay for the loss between the actual and anticipated dates of production. The cover operates from the day on which business would have started but for the damage.

13.22   **Engineering Consequential Loss**
Cover considered so far has been that following fire and perils. Cover in the engineering market works in the same way but there are some differences:

(i)   Cover is in respect of specific machinery and the perils are sudden and unforseen damage and failure of the public utilities (gas, electricity, water or effluent services).

(ii)   There are excesses and franchises applied to the indemnity period to avoid small losses, particularly as a result of temporary breaks in services.

EXAMINATION CONSIDERATIONS
Consequential loss insurance makes very regular appearances in the examinations and the student must know the detail of this subject. In the past, questions have covered general discussion about the nature or desirability of the cover, specific calculations of sums insured as outlined earlier and loss calculations as demonstrated in the Appendix. It is very important to learn this section of the course.

APPENDIX 1

PAST EXAMINATION QUESTIONS

(Reproduced with the kind permission of the Chartered Insurance Institute).

Chapter 1   Introduction

1983 Question 7
A new client who owns a large, sprinklered warehouse from which, utilising his own transport, he supplies his chain of shops which sells newspapers, stationery and books, seeks your guidance on appropriate insurance protection in respect of all facets of his business.

Outline an insurance programme indicating the scope of cover required for all aspects of the business, excluding liability insurance.

The programme should include:
> fire and special perils (stock on a declaration basis)
> theft (probably on a first loss basis)
> sprinkler leakage
> motor fleet for vans and company cars
> fidelity guarantee
> money
> goods in transit
> engineering (if lifts or lifting equipment on site)
> business interruption
> glass insurance.

1985 Question 2 (part g)
Write short notes on The Insurance Ombudsman Bureau.

The Insurance Ombudsman Bureau was set up in 1981 to investigate and, if possible, settle disputes between private policyholders and insurers. The work of the bureau is paid for by insurers and there is no charge to policy-holders. The decision of the IOB is binding on insurers up to £100,000 but is not binding on the insured, who can proceed to arbitration if dissatisfied with the decision.

The dispute must be referred to the Bureau within six months of the date on which the insurer has given a final decision at head office level on the complaint, and the case must be withdrawn from legal proceedings while it is in front of the Ombudsman.

Chapter 2   The Basic Principles

1983 Question 8
The following cases deal with basic principles of insurance.

Discuss the principle enunciated in each case:
> (i)   Carter v Boehm (1766)

56

(ii) Castellain v Preston (1833)

(iii) Tootal Broadhurst Lee Co. Ltd. v London & Lancashire Fire Insurance Co. (1908)

(i) Utmost good faith

(ii) Subrogation and indemnity

(iii) Proximate cause

1985 Question 2 (part d)

Write short notes on Tootal, Broadhurst, Lee Co. Ltd. v London & Lancs (1908).

This concerned a claim for fire damage following an earthquake in Jamaica in 1907. Fire broke out in the premises occupied by Curphey, allegedly due to the earthquake, and spread naturally to burn down the insured building. The policy excluded fire due to earthquake. It was held that as the fire spread naturally, the proximate cause was earthquake and the insured lost the case.

Part c) Write short notes on Warranties (as used in a fire policy).

The express warranties in fire policies are continuing or promissory warranties, in that the insured is required to comply with them throughout the currency of the policy.

A warranty is a stipulation as to the existence or continuance of a certain state of affairs or as to performance or non-performance of some act by the insured. For example — warranted all shavings and othr refuse be swept up and removed from the premises daily.

A warranty must be strictly complied with and if broken, however trivial, entitles the insurer to repudiate the contract irrespective of whether the breach increases the risk or not, or whether the loss is directly due to the breach. In practice, many insurers take a lenient view when they are not unduly prejudiced by the breach.

Part b) Write short notes on Rehabilitation of Offenders Act 1974.

The intention of the Act is to wipe the slate clean after a person has been convicted of a crime of minor severity, paid the penalty, and been convicted of no further offence for a period which varies with the original sentence. After this period the person is entitled to speak or act as if they had neither committed the crime nor been convicted of it. The conviction is said to be spent and there is no obligation to disclose a spent conviction on a proposal form, however worded. Knowledge of a spent conviction will not provide grounds for repudiating a claim.

If another person discloses any information forbidden by the Act, they will be guilty of defamation and will be liable in damages to the defamed person.

1985 Question 8

a) The principle of contribution is enshrined in common law. Identify and comment on the four factors which must exist before it can be applied.

b) How is contribution modified under the conditions of a standard fire policy?

c) What specific action do insurers take by way of policy wordings to prevent dual insurance? Give examples.

d)   An insured who has an all-risk policy and a comprehensive private motor car policy has a personal effects to the value of £40 stolen from his locked car.
  (i)   Give reasons why he may wish to claim under only one policy, stating which one.
  (ii)   What course of action should be taken to avoid possible future contribution?

a)   The four factors which must exist to enable contribution to apply are that both or all policies cover the same peril and the same subject matter, have been effected by or on behalf of the same insured and both policies must be indemnity based.

b)   Contribution under a standard fire policy is modified as follows:
—   the liability of each insurer is limited to its rateable proportion of loss or damage;
—   there is an application of a condition of average if the other insurance policy is subject to such a condition;
—   if the other insurance excludes contribution, then the fire policy is limited to such a proportion of the destruction or damage as the sum thereby insured bears to the total value of the property

c)   Specific action taken to prevent dual insurance is that a household policy excludes property more specifically insured e.g. jewellery under an all-risks policy. Theft policies exclude risks more properly insured under fire or glass policies. Glass policies exclude damage which can be covered under a fire policy. Fire policies exclude property more specifically covered under a marine policy.

d)   i)   He should claim under the all risks policy to avoid loss of NCD. The restricted cover provided by a motor policy may limit the amount of a claim. Items stolen may be excluded from the cover provided by a motor policy. There may be an excess on the motor policy.
  ii)   The insured could ask for the rugs, clothing and personal effects extension to be deleted from his motor policy to avoid possible contribution and loss of NCD.

Chapter 3   Sums Insured, Average Reinstatement, Valued and First Loss Policies

1982 Question 6
A programme consisting of policies providing cover for standard fire and special perils, theft (business premises), insurance of money, engineering and loss of profits is under discussion with a manufacturer. The factory building is leased and the landlord has covenanted to insure the buildings against fire. Advice is sought by the proposer on the following matters:
a)   Need he concern himself about the building insurance?
b)   Is it sufficient to insure plant and machinery under the engineering cover only?
c)   Sums insured and covers have been arranged on a reinstatement basis for fire, special perils and theft. Can the engineering cover be arranged similarly and how should the sums insured for engineering be determined.

Write short notes on the points you would make to the proposer.

a)   The proposer must concern himself with building insurance. Is the sum insured adequate? Is it on a reinstatement basis? Will cover be reinstated after a loss? If the landlord has just insured against fire, the proposer will need special perils cover.

b)   No, because fire is excluded and there will be the need for special perils, theft and consequential loss covers.

c)   Yes. The sum insured must be adequate to replace and install the equipment and pay for damage to surrounding property in certain cases.

1982 Question 8 Part b)

To what extent is the insurer liable to pay claims under each of the following circumstances? Give full reasons for your answers.

b)   Damage assessed at £10,000 occurred under a first loss sprinkler leakage policy with a sum insured of £7,500. The total value of the goods insured was £20,000. The loss was caused by the fracture of a sprinkler pipe due to a severe cold spell over the Christmas shut-down.

This question is **not** about average because we are not told what is the declared full value. The insurer is liable for £7,500 provided there was no neglect by the insured and the severe cold was uncharacteristic.

1983 Question 8 Part a) and c)

a)   Distinguish between the following, indicating in each case the circumstances in which it might be used and the advantages and disadvantages to insured and insurer:

i) a first loss policy   ii) a policy subject to a deductible

c)   Property valued at £10,000 is insured for £7,500 subject to average. Damage occurs to the extent of £120. What payments would be made assuming it was subject to:

i) an excess of £100   ii) a franchise of £75.

a)   A first-loss policy does not represent the full amount at risk and is used where it is anticipated that only a partial loss would ever occur e.g. sprinkler leakage insurance. Advantages are lower liability for the insurer, lower cost for the insured. Disadvantages are that the insured's estimate may be inadequate therefore he would lose and the insurers are disadvantaged by the prospect of a total loss for a smaller premium.

A deductible is a large excess whereby the insured pays for the smaller losses himself e.g. £20,000 deductible on a fire policy. The advantage for the insurer is avoidance of small claims and the insured pays lower premiums. Disadvantage for the insurer is reduced premium whilst still exposed to larger losses.

c)   Assuming it is not the special or 75% condition of average but pro rata, then the calculation is:

$$\frac{£7,500 \times £120}{£10,000} = £90$$

Under (i) nothing is payable; loss = £90   excess = £100.
Under (ii) £90 is payable as it exceeds the £75 franchise.

1984 Question 5

Fire insurers have developed various methods designed to help clients make suitable allowance for the effects of inflation when fixing their sums insured.

a)   Explain in detail the operation of Day One Basis of Reinstatement cover.

b)   Describe briefly one other method generally available.

a)   This sytem allows for a two part sum insured; the declared value and an added provision for inflation. The declared value is updated at each renewal. It is essential that the sum insured is adequate because average applies. The insured does not **select** an inflation rate but the sum insured is increased automatically. The insured can either pay a flat rate of 15% above normal terms or 7.5% above normal terms adjustable at the end of the policy period on the increased declared value.

b)   Under the Escalator Clause the insured chooses a rate of inflation expressed as an annual percentage rate. The sum insured is then increased by that amount over the policy period and a 50% additional premium is payable.

1985 Question 5

Fire insurers are sometimes asked to remove the pro rata condition of average. Explain the advantages and disadvantages to:

a)   The insurer, and

b)   the insured

of deleting the pro rata condition of average from a policy of fire insurance.

a)   The advantages to the insurer are few. Firstly, the responsibility for the cost of valuing all property at risk to determine whether under-insurance exists at time of claim is removed. If the insured is penalised by under insurance in the event of a total loss, he has no grounds to complain about an unfair policy condition or of harsh treatment. Loss settlement is simplified.

The disadvantages to the insurer are that it may lead to the risk of under-insurance either accidently or deliberately as a first loss insurance results in an inadequate premium being obtained. The rate fixing is made more difficult as less accurate statistics are available. It also means partial losses up to total sum insured must be paid in full regardless of the relationship between value at risk and the sum insured. It leads to inevitable complaints if the loss exceeds the sum insured.

b)   The first advantage to the insured is that under-insurance is not penalised. As, in practice, total losses are rare, inadequate recovery in the event of a loss is also rare and premium savings are thus possible. The need for constant adjustment of the sums insured, especially in times of high inflation, becomes much less important. So long as the sums insured are just adequate to provide for the largest risk where there is a multiplicity of risk, there is little risk of inadequate recovery except in the extremely rare event of two or more simultaneous losses.

The disadvantage is that if the sum insured is too low, the loss may exceed the sum insured and if inadequate premiums are received, it may be necessary to increase rates.

1986 Question 2

Write short notes on the following:

c)   Blanket Insurance

There is no division of amounts insured between buildings on the premises. Instead there is one sum insured on each of:
— buildings,
— machinery and plant anywhere on the premises,
— stock floating over the premises.
Each of the above is separately subject to average. The individual average rate charged for the above is based on the various values. The rate holds good for three years, then is re-calculated on the basis of revised declared values. All increases/reductions in the sum insured are calculated at the appropriate average rate. The advantage to the insured is that there is no likelihood of omitting any building or its contents. The advantage to the insurer and the insured is one of simplicity, as the rate is fixed for three years. It is difficult for the underwriter to establish the estimated maximum loss.

e)   Brown v Royal (1859)

This was an action to compel insurers to carry out reinstatement which they had elected to do under a condition of the policy. Work started, but the premises were condemned as dangerous and demolished. The insurers claimed that demolition made reinstatement impossible. The judge decided that the insurers must reinstate or pay damages.

f)   Abitration condition

If there is a dispute over the amount of a claim, the insured must accept arbitration. The making of an award is a condition precedent to any right of action against the insurers. If a dispute is over liability, insurers cannot prevent the insured from suing them. Compared with using the law, arbitration is cheaper, quicker and attracts less publicity.

1986 Question 8

a)   A manufacturer decides to include 'day one' reinstatement cover on the adjustable basis in his new fire insurance policy. The declared value is £1,000,000 and the rate is 0.20%.

i)   What is the provisional premium for the first year?

ii)   If the declared value is increased to £1,200,000 at renewal:
      a)   What is the revised provisional premium;
      b)   What is the additional premium for the previous year

iii) What additional premium is payable on expiry of each period of insurance if the declared value is not submitted to the insurer?

iv)   What would be the sum insured for the declared value of £1,200,000?

b)   A property owner decides to insure his block of flats on the non-adjustable 'day one' basis.

i)   If the declared value on the flats is £2,000,000 and the rate 0.075%, what is the annual premium?

ii) Following a fire in a flat, a claim for reinstatement is made amounting to £5,000. The amount of the estimate is agreed and the work carried out. What form of 'average' would be applied to this claim?

a)

i) Provisional premium

	£1,000,000 @ 0.20%	2000
	Loading 7.5%	150
Provisional premium		£2150

ii) a) Revised provisional premium

	£1,200,000 @ 0.2%	2400
	Loading 7.5%	180
Provisional premium		£2580

b) Additional premium for the previous year:

Provisional premium — Year 2	2580
Provisional premium — Year 1	2150
Difference	430

430 x 50% = £215 additional premium.

iii) An additional premium of 7.5% of the provisional premium becomes payable i.e. £2000 = £150.

iv) The sum insured would be £1,200,000 + 50% = £1,800,000.

b)

i)

	2,000,000 @ 0.75%	=	1500
	Loading 15%	=	225
Annual premium payable			£1725

ii) The form of average applied to this claim would be:

$$\frac{\text{Declared value}}{\text{Actual value on day one}} \quad x \quad \frac{\text{Loss (on reinstatement basis)}}{1}$$

Declared value = Total cost of reinstatement (no deduction for depreciation) plus provision for compliance with public authorities' requirements, professional fees and debris removal. Actual value on the same basis would be assessed by the loss adjuster.

Chapter 4   Risk Reduction and Loss Prevention

1982 Question 5

a)   Insurers accept that a responsibility rests upon them to mitigate and, as far as possible, prevent fire waste. Explain the term 'fire waste' and the methods used by fire insurers to meet this responsibility.

a)   To what extent are theft insurers able to exercise their responsibility for the reduction and prevention of losses?

a)   Fire waste refers to the absolute economic loss of wealth to the community caused by fire. Methods include: rating system, discussion with insured about new buildings, F.P.A., F.I.R.T.O., employment of fire surveyors, advertising.

b)   Theft insurers use rating, warranties, excesses or deductibles, limits in the policy and the employment of theft surveyors. A.B.I.S. is supported as is N.S.C.I.A.

1984 Question 3 Part a)

a)   Describe the underwriting measures and advisory services which are used for risk improvement in the conduct of:

i) fire insurance and ii) fidelity guarantee insurance.

For i) see 1982 a) above. In ii) it is the system of proposal forms (employer's form, employee's form and past employer's form) and the system of check in force. Insurers will ensure an appropriate system is used to reduce the possibility of loss.

1985 Question 2

Write short notes on the following:

a)   The Fire Insurers Research and Testing Organisation (FIRTO) is a company limited by guarantee and financed by the UK fire insurance industry. It examines and tests portable fire extinguishers, automatic fire detection systems, automatic fire extinguishing systems and fire fighting agents, and maintains a test laboratory for fire tests on materials and elements of construction to FOC standards.

1986 Question 2

b)   Write short notes on the following:

The Thatcham project is a research centre set up by the ABI and Lloyd's with the object of controlling the cost and improving the standard of motor vehicle repairs. The centre is based in Thatcham in Berkshire, hence the name. Use is made of a crash simulation rig, the method and time necessary for repair is then carefully monitored. Manufacturers submit cars at the design stage to reduce the cost of repairs. The centre issues reference manuals with recommended repair methods and times. The centre has had great success with 'door skins', substantially reducing the cost of this type of repair.

Chapter 5 Theft Insurances

1984 Question 2

A man effects an 'all risks' travel policy for -£1000 to cover the property of himself and his wife whilst attending a business conference in Spain. On his return he submits a claim for:

a) The cost of a handbag to replace one purchased for the trip which his wife left on a bus — the contents of the handbag included her silver powder compact and the equivalent of £20 in cash. £90.

b) The cost of replacing his wife's evening dress which was sent to be dry-cleaned on their return — the dress is no longer wearable. £25.

c) The cost of a cut-glass decanter to replace one broken in his luggage on the flight home. £50.

d) The cost of a new evening dress suit to replace the suit stolen from his hotel room. £100.

e) The cost of another camera to replace one confiscated by H.M. Customs — the original camera was purchased from his winnings of £200 on the office sweepstake organised during the conference. £230.

f) The cost of a new electric shaver — during the stopover in Northern France he altered the voltage to 110v and failed to alter it back to 240v before using it in Spain, with the result that the motor burned out. £30.

g) The cost of hiring a dress suit to attend a function two days after his return. £30.

Indicate what question you would put to the insured and outline how you would deal with each of these claims. (Ignore any other insurances).

a) This would be covered with the excess applying separately to the cash and to the handbag and compact. Were the police and bus company notified?

b) This is not covered — any process of cleaning, dyeing or restoring is an exclusion.

c) This is not covered, breakage of brittle articles is only covered when caused by fire, theft or attempted theft.

d) This would be covered. Were the police and hotel notified of the loss?

e) This is not covered — property confiscated by H.M. Customs is excluded.

f) This is not covered — electrical or mechanial derangement is an exclusion.

g) This is not covered — cover only applies away from home and ceases upon return. Further this is a consequential loss which would not be covered by most material damage policies.

1984 Question 4

The policyholder, a cafe proprietor, has theft (business premises) and money insurances in force, with sums insured of £7500 and £2000 respectively. He agrees to the Holmesdale Automatic Machine Co. installing six coin-operated 'space invader' machines on the premises, in return for 10% of the takings. He also agrees to empty the machines each night, returning £250 — the float provided by the company — to each machine.

The cafe is broken into one night and two machines have their backs opened up, allowing the thieves access to the float. Whilst attacking the third machine, the thieves are disturbed and make their escape by smashing the plate glass window, The damage to the third machine causes a short circuit in the electrical installation and a small fire occurs.

The cafe proprietor claims:

a) The cost of the repair of the doorway damaged by the break-in by the thieves. £150.
b) The cost of the repair of the machines. £500.
c) The amount of the two floats stolen. £500.
d) The cost of repair of the floor covering damaged by the thieves. £100.
e) The cost of the plate glass window. £200.
f) The cost of cleaning the decorations after the fire. £ 50.

Discuss the liability of the policies for each of the items of the claim.

a) Covered — damaged caused during theft is included in policy cover provided the insured is responsible for repairs.
b) Not covered unless the insured has undertaken to be responsible for them when they will be treated as fixtures and fittings.
c) Not covered — they are not the insured's property and money policies usually exclude the contents of coin-operated machines.
d) Covered — damage caused during theft is included.
e) Not covered — this is a specific exclusion.
f) Not covered — loss or damage by fire is a specific exclusion.

1985 Question 4

a) Discuss the difference between 'theft' as insured in a theft policy relating to business premises and 'theft' under a household policy. Explain clearly why insurers vasry the cover between these two types of policy.
b) What specific exceptions (apart from the general exclusions which appear on most property insurance policies) would you expect to find on a business theft policy?
c) In a business theft policy, under what headings does the property insured normally fall?
d) What other cover, apart from theft of goods from the premises, is normally included in a theft policy?

a) Business premises — The risk covered is generally defined as 'Theft or any attempt thereat, involving entry to or exit from the premises by forcible and violent means', to restrict the wide interpretation of theft under the Theft Act.

Household insurance — Only cash, etc, and theft when the premises are lent, let or sub-let, in whole or in part, are normally subject to the restriction of forcible and violent means, otherwise the full interpretation of the Act applies. The restriction on business premises is to avoid payment for losses due to shoplifting and pilferage, entry by skeleton or duplicate key, entry by trick and secretion unless followed by 'breaking out', but this is wider cover than the insurer is prepared to give. The householder is deemed to exercise control of those who enter his house but, where money is involved, it would be too easy to claim for fictitious losses without the restriction, and for an outsider to steal money through open doors or windows. Similarly, when premises are lent, let or sub-let, control is weakened.

b) Specific exceptions include loss or damage by fire however caused; damage to stained or plate glass or any decoration or lettering thereon; loss or damage by any person lawfully on the premises or directly or indirectly caused or brought about by, or with the connivance of any inmate or member of the insured's household or business staff or any servant of the insured (the collusion risk may be accepted by some insurers on payment of an additional premium); loss of or damage to money, securities, coins, medals, stamps, precious stones or articles composed of any of them, documents, business books, manuscripts, computer systems, records, curios, sculptures, rare books, plans, patterns, models or designs, tobacco, cigars or cigarettes unless specifcally mentioned as insured.

c)   In a business theft policy the property insured falls under the following headings:
—   stock and materials in trade, the property of the insured;
—   property held by the insured in trust or on commission and for which he is responsible;
—   machinery, fixtures, fittings and all contents other than stock and materials in trade.

d)   Cover apart from theft includes any damage occurring to the premises or its contents which is the responsibility of the insured consequent on theft or any attempt thereat.

Chapter 6   Engineering Insurance

1984 Question 7 Part b)
What special considerations have to be taken into account when determining the limit of indemnity on engineering policies covering boiler and pressure vessels?

The sum insured must include the value of the boiler and installation costs, damage to surrounding property and liability for injury to third parties.

1986 Question 2
Write short notes on the following:

a)   Inspection service for engineering insurance.

Under the Factories Act 1961 and the Health and Safety at Work Act 1974, boilers and their related steam vessels and cranes must be thoroughly examined by a competent person at least once in every fourteen months, other lifting devices every six months. The aim of the inspection is to detect defects and arrange correction before damage to the plant and surrounding property occurs. Engineers employed by insurance companies are accepted as 'competent' people and they issue reports to underwriters. Insurers will provide an inspection service without insurance but they will not accept insurance without an inspection. The inspection service only contract is subject to Value Added Tax.

1986 Question 3
In connection with engineering insurance:
a)   Name FIVE types of plant you would expect to find under each of the following headings:
   i)   engine plant
   ii)   lifting machinery
b)   what is the usual definition of 'explosion'?
c)   name two defects in a steam boiler which are not included within the definitions of 'explosion' or 'collapse'.

d) To what extent is it possible for a factory owner to protect himself against the financial after-effects of a machine breaking down?

a) i) Types of plant to be found in an engine plant would include steam engines, gas and oil engines, diesel engines, air compressors, pumps, hydro-extractors, fans, gas producer plant, large refrigerating plant.

ii) Cranes of all types, tractors, dumpers, hooks hoists or teagles, passenger, goods and service lifts, motor vehicle service tables, excavators.

Motive power can be electric, steam, hydraulic, internal combustion or manual.

b) Explosion in engineering insurance means the sudden and violent rending of the plant by force of internal steam or other fluid pressure (other than pressure of ignited flue gases) causing bodily displacement of any part of the plant, together with forcible ejection of the contents.

c) The following defects do not themselves constitute explosion or collapse:
— wearing away or wasting of material of the plant by leakage, corrosion, action of fuel or otherwise;
— slowly-developing deformation or distortion of any part of the plant;
— cracks, fractures, blisters, laminations, flaws or grooving even when accompanied by leakage;
— failure of joints.

d) The factory owner can effect consequential loss machinery breakdown insurance, linked to key machines, to compensate for turnover lost because of the breakdown. The insurance is usually subject to a time franchise. The policy also pays for the increase in the cost of working if it is within the economic limit. Alternatively, the factory owner could effect a 'time-loss' insurance.

Chapters 7 and 8   Fire Insurance

1983 Question 1

The principle of indemnity requires that the insured shall be placed by the insurer in the same pecuniary position after the loss as he occupied immediately before the loss.

Discuss in relation to fire insurance:

a) two extensions of the policy under which the insured can receive an amount MORE than indemnity.

b) three circumstances under which the insured will receive an amount LESS than indemnity.

a) Reinstatement memorandum allows for cost of a new building or new machinery with no deduction for depreciation provided the insured is no better off.

This operates subject to the 85% average rule.

Public authorities clause allows for the additional cost of rebuilding to comply with building legislation or planning requirements.

b) Where average applies to a partial loss because of under-insurance, where an excess, franchise or deductible operates and where the sum insured is inadequate for a total loss.

1984 Question 7 Part a)

When dealing with fire insurance in respect of each of the following types of property, on what basis would a loss settlement be made in order to provide the insured with an indemnity:

i)   retailers' stock in trade ii) farm produce
iii)   machinery   iv) livestock?

i)   Wholesale price plus transport (if any). The selling price would include an element of profit.
ii)   Growing Crops — price at nearest market less the cost of combining, cutting and threshing.
      Corn in stacks — deduct cost of threshing.
      Hay and straw — cost at farm.
iii) Repair cost or estimate of secondhand value or new machinery less allowance for wear, tear and betterment.
iv) Market value at the time and place of fire. If appropriate deduct the value of the carcase.

1985 Question 6

A fire policy covering stock in an electrical goods warehouse has been arranged on a monthly declaration basis. The sum to be insured is £250,000, the rate being £0.16%.
a)   Calculate the provisional premium payable
b)   The following declarations are received:

January	£200,000	July	70,000
February	230,000	August	Nil*
March	250,000	September	Nil*
April	270,000	October	Nil*
May	190,000	November	No declaration
June	160,000	December	200,000

*The insured confirmed that the warehouse was empty whilst new racking was being installed and redecoration was in progress.
Calculate the additional/return premium payable, showing ALL your working.
c)   What was the effect on the sum insured when the stock suffered fire damage amounting to £60,000 on 5 July?

a)   250,000 @ £0.16%   £400
      Less 25%   100

               Provisional premium   £300

b)   April must be reduced to £250,000
November must be shown as £250,000
Each 'nil' counts as a declaration.

Provisional premium paid	£300
Total declarations 1,800,000	
divide by 12 = 150,000 average	
150,000 @ £0.16%	£240
	————
Return premium	£60
	————

Maximum return = one third of provisional premium, i.e. one third of £300 = £100. Therefore repay £60.

c)   The sum insured is not reduced by the amount of the loss, the insured undertakes to pay the appropriate additional premium to renewal.

1986 Question 2

Write short notes on the following:

g)   Public authorities clause — This is an extension to include the additional reinstatement costs of complying, after a fire, with the requirements of the public authorities. It does not cover damage done before the extension was given; where notice has been served on the insured before the damage occurs; expense to which the insured is put for undamaged property or portions of property. It excludes liability for any charge or assessment arising out of capital appreciation. The work must be carried out within twelve months of the damage unless the insurers grant an extension.

1986 Question 6

a)   i)   Outline the various types of 'explosion' which may occur in industry.
     ii)   To what extent is explosion covered in the standard fire policy?
     iii) The usual extension of the fire policy to include explosion has two important exclusions. What are these exclusions in the wording?

b)   i)   Which are the elements of 'riot' which were laid down in Field v Metropolitan Police (1907)?
     ii)   What bearing did the case of J.W. Dwyer Ltd. v Receiver of Metropolitan Police District (1967) have on the recovery by insurers of claim payments for riot damage?

c)   The insured is a tenant on a factory estate and holds adequate fire insurance on the machinery and stock in his factory. Following failure of a thermostat, material undergoing a heating process ignites, causing damage to the machine and other equipment in the factory. The following claim is submitted for the cost of:

i)	materials in the machine, damaged by fire	£250
ii)	replacement of machine	£500
iii)	cleaning down surrounding machines to remove smoke deposit	£750
iv)	cleaning down ceiling and walls to remove smoke deposit	£500

For which claim or claims, if any, is the insurer NOT liable, and why?

a) i)   The types of 'explosion' which may occur in industry include explosion of steam boilers; gas used for trade purposes; flammable gases/liquids; chemicals; dust (flour, rice, sugar etc) and bombs.

ii) Explosion is covered in the standard fire policy for boilers used for domestic purposes only and, in a building not being part of any gas works, of gas used for domestic purposes or used for lighting or heating the building.

iii) The exclusions are for destruction or damage occasioned by the bursting of a boiler, economiser or other vessel, machine or apparatus in which internal pressure is due to steam only and belonging to, and under the control of, the insured. This exclusion has been inserted to avoid overlapping the cover provided by an engineering (boiler) policy. The other exclusion is that for damage or destruction of vessels, machinery or apparatus or their contents resulting from the explosion thereof. This exclusion can be deleted if fire insurers are satisfied that adequate engineering policies have been effected.

b) i)   It was held that the following five elements must be present to constitute a riot.
— the number of people assembled must be not less than three.
— there must be a common purpose.
— there must be an intent to help one another, by force if necessary, against any person who may oppose them in the execution of the common purpose.
— there must be force or violence, not merely used in demolishing, but displayed in such a manner as to alarm at least one person of reasonable firmness and courage.

ii) As a result of this case an assembly must be tumultuous if a recovery is to be made uner the Riot (Damages) Act 1886.

c) The insurer is not liable for materials in the machine. Loss is excluded by '… its undergoing any process involving the application of heat'. The insurer is not liable for cleaning down the ceiling and walls which form part of the building, the insurance of which has presumably been arranged by the landlord.

Chapter 9   Household Insurance

1982 Question 1

a) Explain the methods insurers have used in recent years to combat under-insurance on household policies.

b) As a result of a theft claim under a household policy, it transpires that the full value of the contents is much greater than the sum insured. What options are available to the insurer in dealing with the claim?

a) Minimum premiums, minimum sums insured, index-linking of sums insured, advertising/educational publicity and the application of pro rata average.

b) Policy can be considered void ab initio if under-insurance is severe. Alternatively a compromise settlement could be reached subject to rectification of the sum insured. If the policy had a pro-rata average condition that could be applied. If the policy is on a reinstatement basis, settlement of the claim may be on an indemnity basis.

1983 Question 5

An insured writes to his broker expressing concern about the increase in the number of thefts reported in the newspapers and asking whether his household contents insurance would cover the following events:

i)   Money being stolen from the house by a casual thief who entered through an unlocked kitchen door.
ii)   an overcoat being taken from the coatstand in a restaurant whilst the insured was having a meal.
iii)   theft of personal belongings following a break-in at the home of a friend with whom he was staying for the weekend.
iv)   valuables being forcibly taken from him as he was 'mugged' on the way to the bank to deposit them.
v)   theft of valuables whilst they were in the bank for safe-keeping.

Finally he asks whether, if he installed a burglar alarm system he would benefit from a considerably reduced 'contents' premium. If you were the broker, what answer would you give to these queries.

i)   Not covered — specifically excluded by the policy wording. There must be forcible or violent entry as far as cash is concerned.
ii)   Not covered — only covers theft from a building where the insured resides or works.
iii)   Covered — temporarily removed belongings are covered where the insured is resident.
iv)   Covered — the 'hold-up' risk is covered on journeys to and from a bank.
v)   Covered — but the bank may be responsible as bailee.

An alarm system would be prudent but would not produce a reduction in premium. Conversely Insurers may make a system a prerequisite for granting cover on some risks.

1986 Question 1

a)   The basis of settlement of a claim under any household policies on building and contents is described as 'new for old'.
    i)   What is the reason for this breach of the principle of indemnity?
    ii)   What conditions do insurers insist upon when providing this basis of settlement?
    iii)   To what items within the house would this basis of settlement not apply?

b)   An insured holds a modern household policy on the building and contents of his house, the sums insured being £40,000 and £10,000 respectively; there is no all risks insurance. What is the insurer's liability in the following circumstances:
    i)   The hose from the tap to the washing machine comes apart while the machine is being filled, resulting in water penetrating the kitchen floor into the son's study on the lower ground floor. The claim is submitted for:

Water damage to the ceiling of the study   £135
Water damage to the carpet (it was impossible to remove the stains and had shrunk)
New Carpet   £65
Cost of re-polishing the table   £25
Cost of replacement of textbooks   £35
Cost of oil for paraffin heater installed to dry out the study   £ 5
Cost of dry cleaning the curtains following their fouling by smoke from the faulty paraffin heater   £20

ii)   The insured's wife owns a pendant valued at £750 which, because of its worth, is normally kept in the bank. The item has not been specially mentioned in the policy. The wife decides to wear the pendant at a dinner and collects the pendant from the bank. On the way home her handbag containing the pendant is stolen from her shopping basket. When the handbag is recovered the pendant is missing.

a)   i)   The reason for the breach of the principle of indemnity is that loss settlement is simplified in that the insured is not required to understand the application of indemnity and does not have to make a contribution representing the difference between indemnity and the replacement cost of the article destroyed or stolen. This basis of settlement imposes less of a strain on the relationship between insurer and insured when a loss takes place and more properly represents the insured's expectations of the loss settlement. Competition between insurers has also had a bearing on this development.

ii)   Insurers only provide 'new for old' settlement if in the case of a building policy:
—   the property is maintained in a good state of repair and the sum insured represents the rebuilding cost of the house, and
—   in the case of a contents policy, the sum insured on contents represents the replacement cost as new of the contents of the house.

iii)   This basis does not normally apply to household linen and wearing apparel, although recently even the exclusion of household linen has been dropped by some insurers.

b)   i)   Insurer's liability:
—   water damage to ceiling; provided the house has been properly maintained and the sum insured represents the rebuilding cost of the house, the loss will be paid in full, subject to a full sum insured.
—   carpet, table, textbooks: payable in full, subject to a full sum insured.
—   oil for paraffin heater: payable as the proximate cause of the loss is a peril covered by the policy.
—   curtains fouled by smoke: no liability as the fire has not escaped from its normal confine.
Some household policies do not include 'smoke' as one of the perils covered.

ii)   An extension of the policy normally includes theft of property in the course of removal to or from any bank while in the charge of the insured or a member of his family. It is unusual for a limit of 5% to apply to valuables, unless specifically mentioned. The loss is therefore £10,000 x 5% = £500 = limit of payment.

Chapter 10   Reinsurance

1982 Question 3

a)   Distinguish between i) a surplus reinsurance treaty and ii) a quota share reinsurance treaty, and explain the operation of each.

b)   A thriving medium-sized office is offered 100% of the insurance on a new factory and its contents. The office is already heavily committed on neighbouring property and a block limit applies.

Explain in some detail the alternative approaches to the handling of the new risk which might be taken given the following information:

The sums insured are:	New building	£200,000
	Neighbouring property	£500,000
The limits are:	New building	£ 80,000
	Neighbouring property	£100,000
	Block limit	£120,000

The office has a four line treaty and wishes to leave the present reinsurance on the neighbouring property undisturbed.

a)   Under a surplus treaty reinsurance, the 'surplus' above the insurer's retention is ceded to the reinsurers up to an agreed number of 'lines' each line being equal to the ceding insurer's retention. Under quota share a fixed percentage of every risk of the agreed class accepted by the insurer is ceded to the reinsurers.

b)   Retention on the new insurance must be restricted to £20,000 and the acceptance must be limited to £100,000 (£20,000 net plus 4 lines of £20,000 to surplus reinsurers). Alternative approaches are: if 100% of the insurance is accepted, five lines of facultative reinsurance will be required. If facultative reinsurance is not available the office can accept only 50% of the risk.

1983 Question 2 Part b)
Explain the term 'Underwriting or working excess of loss reinsurance'.

This is non-proportional reinsurance where the cover is arranged in layers. It is mainly used for liability insurance and for the protection of the fire account from major claims. The insurer carries all claims or the part of all claims which fall into the first layer. Reinsurers are responsible for all claims, or a proportion thereof, excluding the first layer. Each layer is exhausted before the next layer is involved. The reinsurer normally provides cover against losses on a per risk basis.

1985 Question 1

a)   Explain briefly what is meant by following terms used in the reinsurance market:
   i)   ceding office
   ii)   a 'line'
   iii) facultative reinsurance.

b)   i)   Can a policyholder derive any benefit from the reinsurance arrangements of his insurer. If so how?
   ii)   In the event of the collapse of the insurer, can an insured seek recovery from the reinsurer. Give your reasons.

c)   An insurer is offered a share of a new collective insurance in respect of a large departmental store and the detached ancillary warehouse. The department store is sprinklered. The sums insured are:

Departmental store	£2,600,900
Warehouse	£ 960,000

The insurer's limit for this class of business is £20,000, the limit being doubled if the premises are sprinklered. The insurer has a ten-line surplus treaty and can secure two lines of facultative reinsurance in respect of the departmental store and one line in respect of the warehouse. What percentage of the schedule could the insurer accept (full working to be shown).

a) i) The office which seeks reinsurance is known as the ceding office.

ii) A 'line' is the ceding office's retention.

iii) With facultative reinsurance each risk is reinsured individually. The reinsurer is free to accept or reject the offer as he judges best. Each reinsurance is a separate contract and renewal must be re-negotiated. Both parties must exercise utmost good faith towards each other. Facultative reinsurance is mainly used to supplement treaty reinsurance arrangements or in circumstances where it is not considered equitable to involve the treaty.

b) i) The insured cannot derive direct benefit from the reinsurance arrangements of an insurer. However, without reinsurance the insurer would be unable to accept a large amount of the risk, and insurance would have to be spread over a number of companies, with great expense all round. Reinsurance also helps to smooth the peaks and troughs of underwriting results and enables the insurer to hold rates and acceptance limits.

ii) The insured is not a party to the reinsurance contract and has no direct right to recovery from the reinsurer. The insured cannot benefit directly, although funds due from the reinsurer will become part of the general assets and may be used in payment or part payment of an outstanding claim.

c)	Departmental Store		Warehouse
Sum Insured	2,600,000		960,000
Limit	40,000		20,000
Acceptance			
—Own Line	40,000		20,000
—Treaty 10 lines	400,000		200,000
—Fac. 2 lines	80,000	1 line	20,000
	520,000		240,000

$$\text{Departmental Store} \quad \frac{520,000}{2,600,000} \quad x \quad \frac{100}{1} = 20\%$$

$$\text{Warehouse} \quad \frac{240,000}{960,000} \quad x \quad \frac{100}{1} = 25\%$$

1986 Question 4

An insurer has been operating a quota share treaty for many years under which 80% of all risks are ceded to reinsurers. The gross acceptance under the treaty is limited to £500,000 for any one risk in category A (very good risks). The reinsurance manager submits a proposal to the Board for a new 10 line surplus treaty to replace the quota share arrangement.

a) i) Summarise the points which would be submitted to the board explaining the operation of the surplus treaty and the likely advantages and disadvantages which will accrue from its use.

ii) If the insurer did not wish to increase his current maximum net liability, what would be his maximum acceptance for a Category A risk under the proposed surplus treaty without resorting to facultative reinsurance?

b) Why might the fire manager effect excess of loss reinsurance in addition to the surplus treaty?

a) i) A surplus treaty, in contrast to a quota share, allows the underwriter to decide (within the terms of the treaty) how much he will retain of his acceptance for his own account, the surplus being reinsured with the offices forming, the treaty. Capacity is normally expressed in 'lines', one line being equivalent to the ceding officer's retention:

For example — 6 line treaty

Retention	5,000
6 lines	30,000
	35,000

Acceptance can therefore by up to seven times the retention. The treaty requires that any surplus above the ceding office's retention must be passed to the treaty insurers, up to the treaty limit. Premiums and losses are paid in proportion to the reinsurance arranged. The advantages are that an underwriter can control retention, increasing or decreasing the amount in accordance with his assessment of the risk. There is usually the ability to accept far greater amounts, without exposing the reserves to any increased extent. Since costs of putting an insurance on the books are fairly static, a large acceptance means that the expenses form a much smaller proportion of the premium. The disadvantages include the greatly increased amount of paperwork as each individual risk has to be assessed and the proportion of premium paid to the reinsurer. There have to be arrangements for the appropriate individual recovery of losses paid by the ceding office. The ceding office would face possible greater exposure to loss.

ii) Net liability under quota share: 500,000 x 20%

	=	100,000
With a ten line treaty — Retention		100,000
10 lines		1,000,000
Maximum acceptance		1,100,000

b) The fire manager could effect catastrophe excess of loss, possibly in layers, to protect the fire account from a catastrophe loss arising from one event, e.g. east coast floods. He could effect excess of loss ratio or stop loss to protect the fire account from a loss ratio — claims — which exceeds a given amount.

premiums.

There is normally an upper limit. Cover is bought but seldom exercised.

Chapter 11   Credit and Legal Expenses indsurance

1984 Question 6

An old established engineering firm previously run on 'family' lines and operating within a fairly local part of England is re-formed with new directors and management. A new machine is developed which quickly becomes a best-seller in the U.K. and abroad with a consequent substantial increase in the workforce. As a broker, your advice is sought on the availability of insurance protection which the firm had not previous felt relevant to their operations against:

a)   The possibility that some customers would fail to meet their contracted financial commitments.

b)   The heavy legal expenses that could be incurred in dealing with any disputes which might arise involving either employees or customers.

Describe the scope of covers available to the firm.

a)   For U.K. credit insurance is available. Cover can be provided by specific amount and whole turnover policies. The imposition of excesses and own retention must be mentioned. For risks abroad the Export Credit Guarantee Department covers losses due to economic or political problems. Private insurers will provide for commercial failure only.

b)   Legal expenses insurance covers the costs of defence of disputes with employees and customers; the cost of defence of criminal prosecution under the Health and Safety at Work Act; the cost of lost earnings of an employee or partner attending court; compensation for damages awarded to an ex-employee for wrongful or unfair dismissal.

1985 Question 2 Part e)

Write short notes on Book Debts Insurance.

Goods sold before the fire or other loss are not part of the reduced turnover after a fire, therefore the inability of the insured to collect debts owing to him because his books have been destroyed is not part of the business interruption cover. Special cover may be arranged to pay for the reconstitution of books to assist the insured in collecting the outstanding amounts and for untraced debts. The insured has to submit a monthly statement of outstanding debts during the period of insurance, and this statement is the basis of the claim. The premium payable is based on the average amount of outstanding debts over the year (similar to stock declaration insurance).

Chapter 12   Fidelity Guarantee & Contingency insurance.

1983 Question 6 Parts a) and b)

a)   In a fidelity policy, what is the 'discovery period'

b)   Distinguish between i) general transhipment bond; ii) general warehouse bond; iii) removal bond.

a)   The discovery period is the period between the act of fraud or dishonesty taking place and its discovery. It is usually limited to not more than six months after the resignation, dismissal, retirement or death of the defaulting employee, not later than three months after the termination of the policy, whichever shall happen first. The object of imposing a time limit for discovery is to prevent stale claims which could be troublesome to investigate and where the insurer's right of recovery might be prejudiced.

b)   A general transhipment bond is a bond for the due transhipment of dutiable goods from one ship to another. Duty would be lost by H.M. Customs and Excise if the goods found their way into the country illegally.

A general warehouse bond protects the proprietor of a bonded warehouse and his sureties, if he fails to observe all the provisions of the law on approved warehouses.

A removal bond is required when it becomes necessary to remove dutiable goods (before duty is paid on them) from one bonded warehouse to another. The bond is, in effect, a guarantee that the goods will arrive safely and that duty lost in the event of any shortage will be paid.

Chapter 13   Business Interruption Insurance

1983 Question 6 Part c)
Outline the cover under an engineering consequential loss policy.

It provides for loss of gross profit/increase in cost of working following:
failure of public utilities (subject to excess or franchise)
sudden or unforseen damage to plant.

1984 Question 8
A manufacturer of ladies' clothing, principally summer wear, has three factories in the Midlands. The firm approach you as their broker regarding their business interruption insurance and ask a) how to arrive at a suitable maximum indemnity period; b) whether there are any extensions of cover which would be relevant to their situation. Draft a reply.

Areas to be investigated include physical hazards; the likelihood of loss occurring; extent of possible damage and areas of risk likely to be involved in one loss.

Interruption features: spread of risk in each premises; the number of factories and their independence; the target risk.

Specialities: special machines, raw materials or particularly skilled workers. The seasonal nature of the business, competition and economic climate in general.

Extensions may include: Suppliers, Customers, Failure of utilities, Denial of Access, Goods in Transit.

1985 Question 3
a)   From the following income and expenditure account, suggest a suitable sum insured for a business interruption policy due to commence on 30 June 1985. The policy is on the difference basis, including payroll, and is to have an indemnity period of 12 months. The specified working expenses are raw materials, packing and carriage. It is anticipated that the 10% increase in turnover and expenditure experienced during the past year will continue for the forseeable future. (All workings to be shown).

Accounts for year ending 30 June 1984

	£		£
Opening stock	20,000	Sales	300,000
Raw materials	102,500	Closing stock	35,000
Packing	5,000		
Carriage	7,500		
Wages	50,000		
Salaries	25,000		
Standing charges	53,500		
Net profit	71,500		
	335,000		335,000

b)   The proposer is concerned that the sum insured suggested in a) will be subject to average.
    i)   What alternative policy would you suggest?
    ii)   What gross profit figure would you recommend for such a policy?
    iii) What do you consider to be the advantages to the policyholder of the policy you suggest?

a)   Sum insured on difference basis

Turnover	300,000		
Closing stock	35,000		335,000
Opening stock	20,000		
Raw materials	102,500		
Packing	5,000		
Carriage	7,500		135,000
Basis for sum insured			200,000
To bring up to date		+ 10%	20,000
Year of insurance		+ 10%	220,000
			22,000
			242,000
Indemnity period—12 months		+ 10%	24,200
			266,200

Suggest £280,000 (bearing in mind the return of premium clause and the need to include an amount to cover professional accountants' charges).

b)   i)   The alternative policy would be declaration linked business interruption insurance.
    ii)   £242,000 would be the recommended figure.
    iii) The advantages would be no average, no need to project beyond the period of insurance for inflation, business trends etc, lower initial premium, insured

only pays for the cover actually used, automatic reinstatement of the sum insured after a loss, and generous limit of liability (133.33% of gross profit figure).

1986 Question 2 Part d)
Write short notes on Advance Profits Insurance.

The insured may suffer a financial loss if a new factory or a major extension is damaged by fire or other insured peril before the completion date. Machinery may be damaged or delayed due to fire at a supplier's premises or in transit. An advance profits insurance policy provides cover for the loss due to delay in the use of the new building or an increase in the cost of working to get the building into use in time, or a combination of both.

1986 Question 7
In connection with business interruption insurance:
a) i)   What is the normal definition of 'turnover'?
    ii) What factors govern the choice by the insured of the length of the 'maximum indemnity period'.
    iii) An insured decides to increase the maximum indemnity period under this policy from 12 to 18 months. What effect would this change have on the sum insured and the premium?
b) Following a fire calculate the loss payable from the following information. The policy is a 'declaration linked' business interrtuption insurance with an estimate gross profit for the current year of insurance of £160,000. The loss adjuster obtains the following figures from the insured's accountants:

turnover in previous financial year	£320,000
gross profit in previous financial year	£160,000
standard turnover	£100,000
turnover in the indemnity period	£ 40,000
increase in cost of working (which prevented a loss of turnover of £11,000)	£ 6,000
savings	£ 7,500

The loss adjuster accepts that, because a competitor has gone out of business, an upward trend of 20% is justified.
c) Under a 'declaration linked' business interruption insurance, explain how the insurer receives the true premium for the cover period.

a) i)   Turnover is the money paid or payable for goods sold and delivered and for services rendered in the course of the business at the premises.
    ii) Factors which govern the choice of the length of the indemnity period include the nature of the business, the ability to obtain other premises, the facility with which the existing premises or their contents (machinery, etc) can be repaired or replaced, time taken for customers and trading to be restored to the 'would have been' level and whether the business is seasonal or otherwise.
    iii) An increase in the indemnity period from 12 to 18 months would mean that the sum insured would be increased by 50%. The percentage of the basis rate (multiplier) would be reduced from 150% to 140%. In the event of loss, the annual turnover would be increased by 50%.

b)   Rate of gross profit.

$$\frac{\text{Gross profit}}{\text{Turnover}} = \frac{160,000}{320,000} = 50\%$$

Loss of gross profit:

Standard turnover	100,000	
Trend 20%	20,000	
	120,000	
Achieved	40,000	
	80,000 x 50%	40,000

Increase in cost of working:
6000 spent to avoid a
shortage of turnover of

	11,000	
Economic limit 11,000 x 50% Pay	5,500	
	45,500	
Savings	7,500	
	38,000	

Policy is on declaration linked basis
    — No average applies   Pay   38,000

c)   The insured pays a provisional premium based on the insured's estimate of the gross profit for the financial year most nearly concurrent with the period of insurance. Within six months of the end of the policy year, the insured must provide details to enable the actual earned gross profit to be calculated. Insurers charge an additional premium if the provisional premium has been exceeded or refund premium up to 50% of the premium paid if the earned gross profit is less than the estimated gross profit.

060 APPENDIX 2

THE CHARTERED INSURANCE INSTITUTE

QUALIFYING EXAMINATION

APRIL 1989

SUBJECT 060

Property and pecuniary insurances

Three hours are allowed for this paper. Answer SIX questions only. All questions carry equal marks.

1.   (a) Outline the advantages and disadvantages to both the insured and the insurer of:
     (i) a first loss policy;
     (ii) a policy subject to a deductible,
     and indicate the circumstances in which each might be used.

     (b) Property valued at £16,000 is insured for £12,000. A loss occurs totalling £1,200. What payment would be made under a policy if it were:
     (i) subject to average;
     (ii) subject to the special condition of average?

     In EACH case, how would:
     (i) an excess of £100;
     (ii) a franchise of £100,
     affect the claim payment?

2.   (a) What underwriting factors shoule be considered when cover is required for goods-in-tansit insurance?

     (b) Apart from the standard exclusions of war risks, radio-active contamination and sonic bangs, name SIX exclusions which would appear in a money policy.

     (c) What is the cover provided by a contractors "all risks" policy?

SA 68   81   P.T.O.

3.   An insured holds the following policies relating to his business as a restaurant owner:

Standard fire;
Business interruption;
Theft;
Money;
Glass.

Discuss to what extent each of the following incidents is covered by any of these policies.

(a) A fire in the kitchens damages both buildings and contents and causes the gas boiler used for heating the building to explode, which results in further damage.

(b) As a consequence of the above, there is a 30% reduction in receipts in the three months following the damage, when compared with the three months immediately before the damage.

(c) £500 is found to be missing when an audit is carried out two weeks after an employee left the business.

(d) A person leaves after having a meal in the restaurant and takes some valuable cutlery.

(e) The glass shop front is smashed by vandals. There is no salvage value and the insured requests an immediate cash payment of £600.

(f) A dust explosion in the factory next door damages the insured's premises and causes a fire, the smoke from which contaminates some of the stock. It also shorts the electric cable to the deep freeze cabinet resulting in deterioration of the foodstuffs kept in the cabinet.

4.   Write short notes on FIVE of the following:
(a) credit insurance;
(b) a collective fire policy;
(c) Becker v Marshall (1922);
(d) Association of British Insurers;
(e) court bonds;
(f) excess of loss reinsurance;
(g) F.I.R.T.O.

25

5. A fire policy covering stock in a fancy goods warehouse has been arranged on a monthly declaration basis.

   The sum insured is £240,000 and the rate 0.4%.

   (a) Calculate the provisional premium payable.

   (b) The following declarations are received:

January	£130,000	July	£40,000
February	£110,000	August	Nil*
March	£100,000	September	Nil*
April	£90,000	October	£280,000
May	No declaration	November	£160,000
June	£80,000	December	£130,000

   *The Nil declarations for August and September are confirmed as being correct following a substantial rundown of stock to empty the warehouse before restocking with up-to-date goods ready for Christmas and the January sales.

   Calculate the premium adjustment, showing ALL your workings.

   (c) What would be the effect on the sum insured if a fire on 31 March caused a stock loss of £50,000 and what action would the insured be entitled to take?

6. *(a)* In business interruption insurance what general consequential losses are outside the scope of the policy cover?

   Can insurance be arranged against any of these losses? If so, explain how.

   (b) A client who has the lease of a shop in a modern shopping mall approaches you, his broker, for advice on the need for business interruption insurance.

   The client discloses that 75% of his stock comes from one supplier and that he has a special arrangement to sell one-third of his goods to one customer.

   (i) Draft your reply.
   (ii) State, in an appendix to your reply, any extensions of cover you would recommend, and why.

7. *(a)* Explain the benefits of the inspection service provided by an engineering insurer.

    (b) What underwriting considerations arise when assessing a risk for engineering business interruption insurance?

    (c) Name FOUR common causes of crane breakdown.

8. In connection with 'reinstatement' under a fire insurance policy:

    (a) (i) what is provided under the reinstatement memorandum?

    (ii) what limitations are imposed by this memorandum?

    (iii) to what class of property does the reinstatement memorandum not apply and why is this?

    (iv) what is the advantage to the insured of this form of loss settlement?

    (b) what is the resinstatement option?

    (c) name THREE forms of inflation protection which are available.

    (d) adjust the following loss on a fire policy issued with the reinstatement memorandum and covering buildings, plant and machinery.

	Sum insured	Reinstatement value at time of reinstatement	Loss
Buildings	£110,000	£120,000	£20,000
Plant and machinery	£80,000	£100,000	£40,000

CII examination report 1988 *060*

This report, prepared by the CII's examiners, is intended to help students and teachers in preparing for the examinations by giving an indication of the points which should have been brought out in answers and also examiners' comments on how candidates actually performed in the examinations.

The report shows the main points or headings which examiners were seeking in answer to each question (candidates would be expected to expand upon these points). These are not model answers and should not be regarded as such. There may not indeed be any right or wrong answer to some of the questions, so in cases where candidates displayed imagination and originality, examiners gave them credit even though the answers were not along the lines expected.

Great care is taken in the setting of all papers. For each subject there is a senior examiner who is required to present the paper he has set to a panel of experts and an assessor. Each paper is carefully scrutinised to ensure that there are no ambiguities, errors or inconsistencies and that the paper is generally fair. Assessors and examiners are carefully selected from the insurance industry for their technical expertise and experience and they must be sympathetic to the educational philosophy of the Institute and the needs of the students. The Institute cannot enter into any correspondence about the suggested main points for the answers.

CII Tuition Service study courses include a copy of the latest report. Other 1988 reports can also be obtained separately and most of the 1987 reports are still available; the cost is £1.10 a copy.

ARRANGEMENT

All matter reproduced from the question paper itself is enclosed in boxes. The examiners' comments appear in italic type. First there is a general comment upon candidates' overall performance. Each question is then treated separately: the question itself is printed in a box, then a brief statement of the points that the examiners expected candidates to deal with in their answers, and finally, in italic type, the examiners' comments on how well candidates answered that particular question in the examination.

---

060. Property and pecuniary insurances

Three hours are allowed for this paper. Answer SIX questions only. All questions carry equal marks.

The perennial problem - failure to read the question - was again evident this year. Examples were in question 1 where candidates were asked to OUTLINE the cover, in question 5(b) the reference to ITEMISED blanket insurance and in question 7(b) to BLANKET proposal.

Again, business interruption questions were not popular, questions 1 and 6 being either avoided or producing poor answers.

Questions 3, 7 and 8 however, earned high marks, so that the overall level of marks obtained was similar to previous years.

It was disappointing to find that although 'Day One' and 'Declaration Linked Business Interruption Insurance' have been available for a number of years, the important points of these covers are not fully understood or appreciated.

The attention of teachers and students is drawn to the fact that Motor is no longer part of the syllabus. In consequence, the scope of this paper has been narrowed and subjects such as business interruption, fidelity guarantee etc., will feature more prominently in future papers.

Students who had studied conscientiously appeared to encounter few problems with the paper; this, together with a logical presentation of their answers, enabled them to obtain high marks.

QUESTION 1

Outline and distinguish between the cover afforded by the following insurances in providing protection for pecuniary losses:

(a) business interruption;
(b) book debts.

(a) Business Interruption
  - Protects loss of future income.
  - Designed to deal with the effect which destruction or damage by an insured peril at the insured's premises has on his income.
  - Provides payment for loss of Gross Profit (Standing charges, payroll and net profit).
  Basic perils
  Fire
  Lightning
  Explosion of - domestic boilers
                  - any other boilers or economisers on the premises

- gas used for domestic purposes or for lighting or heating the building.

Special perils can be added.

Extensions to:
- suppliers
- customers
- utilities
- prevention of access

No cover unless material damage proviso is complied with.
Sum insured and rating depend on length of maximum indemnity period.
Policy can be adjustable with initial provisional premium.

(b) Book debts
- Protects loss of income already earned.
- In the event of the destruction of insured's books of account by accident or theft, it will be impossible to prepare statements of outstanding debts due from customers.

Book debts insurance will pay for:
(i) The expenditure incurred in tracing and establishing debit balances (once the debt has been established, it becomes the insured's responsibility to obtain payment).
(ii) The amount of the untraced debts.

The insured is required to provide a monthly statement of outstanding debts. A provisional premium is paid initially and an adjustment, based on the average total of outstanding debts, is made at the end of twelve months. Premium is based on steps taken to preserve the records.

(a) The simple request to outline the cover afforded by a business interruption was usually ignored. In many cases, candidates went to some lengths to explain the calculation of either a loss settlement or the indemnity period. Only occasionally was reference made to the protection of future loss of earnings or to the insured perils, rating or extensions of cover. No attempt was made to distinguish business interruption from book debts cover.

(b) Few made reference to the insurer paying for the cost of tracing the debts. Most candidates thought that the insurer would simply pay for all the outstanding debts (presumably based on the last declaration, but rarely mentioned) without any attempt to trace or recover them. In a number of cases credit insurance was described. Perils were stated as being the 'fire' perils.

Generally a poorly answered question.

QUESTION 2

As a broker placing a large fire schedule on the reinstatement basis, you feel that the insurance of the factory should be on a 'day one' basis.

Explain to your client:

(a) what is meant by 'declared value';
(b) how the premium under the 'adjustable basis' is calculated;
(c) how average would be applied;
(d) why you are recommending this change in the insurance arrangements.

(a) 'Declared value' is the total cost of reinstatement viz:
 (i) re-building and re-equipping the premises in a condition equal to but not better or more extensive than its condition when new (this means no deduction for depreciation); plus
 (ii) due allowance for:
 - the additional cost of reinstatement to comply with Public Authority requirements;
 - professional fees;
 - debris removal costs.
 All the above are calculated as on the first day of insurance year.

(b) The initial premium is loaded by $7\frac{1}{2}\%$.
 At renewal, an additional premium of 50% of the difference between the renewal premium (loaded by $7\frac{1}{2}\%$) and the initial premium is charged.

(c) $$\frac{\text{Declared value}}{\text{Actual value calculated as in (a) above on 'Day One'}} \times \text{Loss}$$

(d) Underwriters provide cover for 150% of 'Declared Value'. This should be sufficient to cover the cost of reinstatement, even if reinstatement is not completed until $2\frac{1}{3}$ years after the insurance was arranged.

(a) The word 'declared' was sufficient inducement for some candidates to refer to stock declaration insurances. Other common faults were not to refer to the fact that this related to reinstatement insurances or that the value was that applying on 'Day One'.

(b) This part of the question was well understood.

(c) Again the constant omission of reference to the values at 'Day One' was apparent. In addition, many candidates referred to 85% reinstatement average.

(d) Most candidates considered that a simple reference to inflation protection was all that was required. Not many answers referred to the extent of the protection.

The answers were, on the whole, just about adequate.

QUESTION 3

An office is offered a share of a collective fire insurance covering a large furniture manufacturing risk, of which only the main factory is sprinklered.

The sums insured by the three items of the schedule are:

Timber yard	Stock	£280,000
Main factory	Bldgs/Mchy/Stk	£1,000,000
Finished goods warehouse	Bldgs/Mchy/Stk	£480,000

All are separate risks.

The office limits its retention for this class of risk to a maximum sum insured of £20,000, this retention being doubled for sprinklered risks. The office has a five line surplus treaty and an agreement with another office to provide facultative cover equivalent to one line on the timber yard, two lines on the finished goods store and four lines on the factory.

(i) What is the maximum percentage which the office could accept? (Full calculations to be shown)

(ii) What percentage is it likely to accept, and why?

Timber yard — £280 000

1 line retained	20 000
5 line surplus treaty	100 000
1 line facultative	20 000
Maximum acceptance	140 000

$$\frac{140\ 000}{280\ 000} \times \frac{100}{1} = 50\%$$

Main factory — £1 000 000

1 line retained	40 000
5 line surplus treaty	200 000
4 line facultative	160 000
Maximum acceptance	400 000

$$\frac{400\ 000}{1\ 000\ 000} \times \frac{100}{1} = 40\%$$

Finished Goods — £480 000

1 line retained	20 000
5 line surplus treaty	100 000
2 line facultative	40 000
Maximum acceptance	160 000

$$\frac{160\ 000}{480\ 000} \times \frac{100}{1} = 33\tfrac{1}{3}\%$$

(i) Maximum acceptance - $33\tfrac{1}{3}\%$

(ii) Likely acceptance - not more than 30% to allow for increases in sum insured.

Some candidates added the individual risk acceptances together to produce a maximum acceptance for the policy. Others stated that the insurer could accept the individual proportions for each part of the risk, completely missing the point that, as a collective policy was involved, the finished goods warehouse governed the maximum acceptance for the insurer. Another common mistake was to reduce the acceptance amount because the trade was hazardous, although the question clearly refers to the retention for this class of risk.

Where candidates understood the principle of the collective policy, high marks were obtained.

QUESTION 4

Write short notes on FIVE of the following:

(a) engineering business interruption insurance;
(b) Loss Prevention Council;
(c) Rehabilitation of Offenders Act 1974;
(d) The Insurance Ombudsman Bureau;

(e) special condition of average;
(f) bankruptcy bond;
(g) long term agreements.

(a) Engineering business interruption insurance

Similar to a normal business interruption insurance, but perils insured under a fire B/I policy are usually excluded. Insurance is linked to **breakdown** of specified machines or plant. There is usually a time excess. The indemnity period is usually short. Failure of public utilities can be included.

(b) The Loss Prevention Council

Continues the technical work previously undertaken by the Fire Offices' Committee.
The LPC consists of:
> The Association of British Insurers;
> Lloyd's;
> The FOC Technical Services;
> The Fire Insurers' Research and Testing Organisation;
> The Fire Protection Association.

The LPC administers Loss Prevention schemes through the Loss Prevention Certification Board.

(c) The Rehabilitation of Offenders Act 1974

The effect of the Act is that certain criminal convictions are deemed to be 'spent' after a period of time. After this period, a person is entitled to speak and act as if he had neither committed the crime nor been convicted of it. Insurers may not repudiate a claim where a spent conviction has not been disclosed to them. A person who discloses information forbidden by the Act is guilty of defamation and will be liable in damages to the defamed person.

(d) The Insurance Ombudsman Bureau

Set up in 1981 to investigate and attempt to settle disputes between **private** policyholders and insurers who are members of the bureau. The cost is met by the member insurers - there is no charge to the policyholders. IOB decisions are binding on member insurers up to £100,000 but not binding on policyholders, who, if dissatisfied, can proceed to arbitration or other legal action. Disputes must be referred to the Bureau within six months of the date on which the member insurer makes a final decision on the claim at Head Office level. There must be no legal proceedings while the case is before the IOB.

(e) Special Condition of Average

Mainly used in insurances of agricultural products and ecclesiastical risks. If the sum insured is greater than 75% of the value at risk at the time of the loss, the condition does not apply. If the sum insured is less than 75%, pro rata average will apply. (Note: Candidates would be expected to provide an example of the operation of this condition.)

(f) Bankruptcy Bond

A bankrupt's property is transferred to a trustee in bankruptcy appointed by the creditors. Before the appointment is confirmed, the trustee must obtained a certificate of appointment from the Department of Trade. The Department will not issue the certificate until security is given. A bond by an insurance company is the usual security. The Bond is in favour of the Department of Trade and secures the proper carrying out by the trustee of his duties.

In case of failure by the trustee, the Surety (the insurer):
- makes good to the estate any loss or damage;
- pays any sums for which the trustee may be liable by way of interest;
- pays certain costs in connection with the removal of the defrauding trustee and the appointment of a new one.

The bond continues in force until discharged by the Department of Trade

(g) **Long Term Agreements**

Where the insured agrees to offer to renew the policy for three years and signs an agreement to this effect, the insurers undertake to allow a discount of 5% off the annual premium. Insurers are under no obligation to renew the policy. If the rates are increased or additional terms are imposed, the insured is not obliged to renew the policy. The insured may reduce the sums insured at any time to correspond with any reduction in the value of the property insured.

(a) Engineering B/I - the perils were rarely mentioned or if mentioned, it was usually 'fire perils' or failure of public utilities - machinery breakdown was seldom referred to.

(b) LPC - candidates constantly referred to provision of loss prevention information and literature, but there was little reference to the constituent parts of the Council.

(c) Rehabilitation of Offenders Act 1974 - this was well understood, though several candidates thought the Act applied only to insurance contracts.

(d) Insurance Ombudsman Bureau - few references were made to PRIVATE policyholders and some candidates confused the IOB with the arbitration condition and its advantages (as occurred with PIAS last year). Also persistent reference to claims disputes as being the only matters handled by the IOB.

(e) Special Condition of Average - this was well understood.

(f) Bankruptcy Bonds - understood in general terms, but few references made to the Dept. of Trade requirements for such bonds before the certificate is issued.

(g) Long term agreements - no real problem, although sometimes related to long term insurances.

A popular question, usually well answered, although LPC and Bankruptcy Bonds were not often chosen for answer.

QUESTION 5

(a) Factory contents are insured under a material damage fire policy extended to include sprinkler leakage on a 'first loss' basis for £50,000, subject to the usual first loss average wording.

The declared value is stated to be £800,000.

A claim, following a fractured sprinkler pipe, is

---

submitted for:

(i)	– damage to machinery	£25,000
(ii)	damage to stock	£20,000
(iii)	repairs to sprinkler piping	£9,000
(iv)	clearing up	£500
(v)	two days' loss of production	£13,500

The amounts involved are verified, subject to the insured contributing £150 in respect of the machinery item and £350 in respect of some salvage of stock.

Owing to the insured's involvement in a new overseas order, it was found that the actual value at risk in respect of contents of the factory was £900,000.

Adjust the claim.

(b) (i) As a broker, explain to your client the key features of an itemised 'blanket insurance' as applied to a manufacturer's premises - buildings, machinery and stock.

(ii) What are the advantages, if any, to the client in placing his insurance on this basis?

(iii) What problems does such an insurance present to the underwriter?

(a) (i)	Machinery	25 000	
	less	150	24 850
(ii)	Stock	20 000	
	less	350	19 650
(iv)	Clearing up		500
			45 000

(iii) and (v) not covered

$$\frac{800\ 000}{900\ 000} \times 45\ 000 = 40\ 000$$

(b) (i)
- One sum insured on all buildings.
- One sum insured on machinery anywhere on the premises.
- One sum insured on stock floating over the whole of the premises.
- Each sum insured is separately subject to average.
- One average rate for each of buildings/machinery/stock.
- Rates are held for three years. All increases and reductions in sums insured are calculated at the appropriate average rate.
- At the end of the three years the rates are recalculated.

(ii) Advantages to client:
- Simplicity - all buildings/machinery/stock automatically included - no buildings or items of machinery omitted.
- Since rates are fixed, the client can budget the cost of insurance for new buildings and their contents.

(iii) Problems for the underwriter:
- Difficulty in applying average in the event of a loss.
- Scarce information regarding location and extent of maximum values, making it difficult to estimate the extent of any probable loss - hence lower acceptance and retention.
- Complicated average rate calculation.

(a) Candidates often applied average to each item of the claim and deducted 'savings' from the final total. However, this part of the question was generally well understood.

(b) (i) Reference to an 'itemised blanket insurance' was ignored by many candidates, who referred to a single sum on buildings, machinery and stock. Reference was seldom made to an average rate calculation or holding rates for three years, with a recalculation. In other cases, reference was made to blanket cover meaning 'all risks' or a combined policy.

(ii) Simplicity was the answer usually provided. There was no reference to budgeting for future premium costs. An advantage to clients was sometimes stated as being that the insurer would find it difficult to apply average.

(iii) Difficulty in applying average was the problem most candidates appreciated. Few candidates mentioned EML, or the rate calculation.

Not a popular question; only 50% of the candidates attempted it and part (b) was not particularly well answered.

QUESTION 6

Underwriters have been concerned that loss settlements under business interruption policies have been reduced owing to inadequate sums insured.

What steps have underwriters taken to provide an insurance to meet this problem?

Declaration Linked Business Interruption Insurance.

Insurers require the insured to provide an 'Estimated Gross Profit' sum insured for the forthcoming year of insurance, for which a provisional premium is charged.

Insurers hold covered for $133\frac{1}{3}\%$ of this figure, which is the 'limit of liability'.

All losses up to this limit are paid in full. Proportionate reduction (average) does not apply.

When accounts which most nearly coincide with the insurance year are published, the insured submits a certificate of the actual Gross Profit earned in the year of insurance to enable the true premium to be calculated. The maximum return of premium is 50% of the provisional premium; there is no upper limit to the additional premium.

The insurance also includes provision for the automatic reinstatement of the sum insured, to protect the insured in the event of a further claim or claims in the same insurance year.

Those candidates who attempted this question spent most of the answer explaining why it was difficult to calculate future Gross Profit and, in many cases, then referred to material damage methods of combatting inflation (NRVS etc.). Others solely referred to the Rebate Clause. Those candidates who did refer to Declaration Linked Business Interruption insurances usually produced a reasonable answer, but overall this was not a particularly well answered question, nor popular as only about one in three candidates attempted it.

QUESTION 7

In connection with fidelity guarantee insurance:

(a) describe three types of policy which may be issued;
(b) what information would you expect to find in a blanket proposal form?
(c) what additional information would you require where a computerised system operates?

(a) - Individual policy - one employee for a stated amount.
- Named Collective policy - schedule of names and duties with an amount against each name, or a floating sum.
- Unnamed Collective policy - employees covered by category, with an amount per capita or a floating sum.
- Blanket policy - unnamed collective policy including all employees with floating sum.
- Positions policy - used for local government, where the 'position' is guaranteed for a specific amount.

(b) - Nature of business.
- System of supervision.
- Enquiries made by an employer before engaging staff.
- The number of employees having responsibility for money and/or stock:
    - indoor employees;
    - outdoor employees.
- The number of employees not having responsibility for money and/or stock:
    - office staff;
    - others.
- Claims history.

(c) - Is there an independent check of completed programs and/or modules and if so, how often?
- Can the program be run by a single operator?
- Do systems analysts and data preparation operators have access to the computer room?
- Is anyone responsible for data protection allowed access to control records?
- How are program changes authorised and records of changes kept?
- Is a self-checking system incorporated for internal control?
- Is there a rotational system for operational duties?
- What functions do external auditors exercise in connection with the system?

(a) Few candidates made mention of the amount of the guarantee or to whom it would apply, but otherwise this part of the question was well answered.

(b) A number of candidates went to great lengths to explain what information appeared on an individual employees's proposal form, despite the question referring to a blanket proposal.

(c) Answers to this part of the question were usually good, although inclined to be long-winded.

No real problem with this question, which was usually well answered, with a number of candidates earning full marks

QUESTION 8

(a) What is the definition of 'theft' in the Theft Act 1968?

(b) (i) In what way is cover for theft limited in theft insurance policies on business premises?

    (ii) Explain the reasons for this amendment.

(c) Outline the features of a risk on which you would expect a theft surveyor to comment.

(a) Definition of theft.

- A person is guilty of theft if he dishonestly appropriates property belonging to another with the intention of permanently depriving the other of it, and 'thief' and 'steal' shall be construed accordingly.
- It is immaterial whether the appropriation is made with a view to gain, or is made for the thief's own benefit.

(b) Theft is defined as:

(i) Theft involving entry to or exit from the building by forcible and violent means.

(ii) The intention of the insurers is to cover the loss of property which results from the breaking down of the defences. The insurers do not wish to cover losses following:
- use of key, whether original, duplicate or skeleton;
- entry by a trick;
- shop lifting or pilferage by staff;
- entry by a thief legitimately, who then secretes himself inside, unless the thief makes his exit by forcible and violent means.

(c) Features of a risk on which the theft surveyor would be expected to comment:
- construction of premises;
- areas and situation of risk;
- surroundings;
- security:
  - locks, bolts and bars,
  - window fastenings,
  - alarm details,
  - safe details;
- occupation / type of business carried on;
- attractiveness of contents;
- amounts of attractive contents at risk;
- amount of cash kept on the premises and in safe overnight;
- method of securing the premises at night and keyholder(s);
- risk improvements required;
- warranties;
- claims.

(a) This was usually well known and understood.

(b) Both parts relating to the limitation of theft were well understood.

(c) Answers to this part of the question were usually good, although inclined to be long-winded.

This was a very popular question, answered well in most cases, and earned good marks.

INDEX